BIBLE TRIVIA
CHAL

MATCH 'EM

*Can You Make
the Right Connection?*

ELLEN CAUGHEY

BARBOUR
PUBLISHING

For Ellen
Here's to road trips with weigh stations. . .
and our special friendship.

Published by Barbour Publishing, Inc., P.O. Box 719, Uhrichsville, Ohio 44683, www.barbourbooks.com

Our mission is to publish and distribute inspirational products offering exceptional value and biblical encouragement to the masses.

Member of the
Evangelical Christian
Publishers Association

Printed in the United States of America.
5 4 3 2 1

CONTENTS

INTRODUCTION

You can match outfits, funds, and, of course, socks. . .but are you ready to *match wits*? Welcome to *Bible Trivia Challenge: Match 'Em*, where matching (there's that word again!) is the only way to uncover the correct answers.

Here's a sneak preview: sixty quizzes with intriguing titles, designed to plumb the depths of your knowledge of the Bible. . .ten questions in each quiz, with each one increasingly, no, make that maddeningly, more difficult . . .600 questions in all, with a mind-boggling total of 330,000 points for a perfect score!

Match 'Em is as simple as matching one of three "Match Group" entries with a "Match Word," and as challenging as knowing who was in jail with Paul at Philippi, on what day of Creation birds came into being, and just how many years Solomon spent building God's temple! Every tenth quiz is a Who's Who of all those major and minor players you thought you knew. . .hmm, was that Zipporah or Zeresh? And that's all the help you're going to get.

Each question is worth from 100 to 1,000 points, with a perfect score, per quiz, of 5,500 points. Keep score as you go by entering your totals in the spaces provided following the quizzes. Answers to all *Match 'Em* quizzes follow the final quiz and include the appropriate scripture citations. All scripture references, as well as any explanatory notes, are from the New International Version of the Bible, unless otherwise indicated.

Get ready to match wits as you *Match 'Em*!

Quiz I:
Who's Who
Part I

1. (100 pts.)
MATCH WORD: Luke

MATCH GROUP
a. Original apostle of Jesus
b. Tax collector
c. Wrote two books of the Bible to Theophilus

2. (200 pts.)
MATCH WORD: Jethro

MATCH GROUP
a. Moses' father-in-law
b. Moses' son by Zipporah
c. Aaron's father-in-law

3. (300 pts.)
MATCH WORD: Orpah

MATCH GROUP
a. Sister of Boaz
b. Sister-in-law of Ruth
c. Daughter of Naomi

4. (400 pts.)
MATCH WORD: Vashti

MATCH GROUP
a. Another name for Esther
b. Queen of Persia
c. Mordecai's cousin

5. (500 pts.)
MATCH WORD: Apollos

MATCH GROUP
a. Fervent preacher in the early church
b. Tentmaker who aided the apostles
c. Greek silversmith

MATCH 'EM

6. (600 pts.)
MATCH WORD: Ehud

MATCH GROUP
a. Killed Eglon, king of Moab
b. Followed Samson as judge of Israel
c. Commander of Jabin's army

7. (700 pts.)
MATCH WORD: Drusilla

MATCH GROUP
a. Sister of Herod Agrippa II
b. Wife of Felix, governor of Judea
c. Wife of Pontius Pilate

8. (800 pts.)
MATCH WORD: Jehoiakim

MATCH GROUP
a. King who fled from the Babylonians against Jeremiah's advice
b. King of Babylon
c. King who burned Jeremiah's scrolls

9. (900 pts.)
MATCH WORD: Jotham

MATCH GROUP
a. Proclaimed himself king of Shechem
b. Only brother to escape Abimelech's wrath
c. Last judge of Israel

10. (1,000 pts.)
MATCH WORD: Baruch

MATCH GROUP
a. Wrote Jeremiah's words on a scroll
b. With Deborah, was a judge of Israel
c. Accompanied Paul on his first missionary journey

Quiz 1 Total Points: _____

Quiz 2:
fishers of Men

1. (100 pts.)
MATCH WORD: Number of the disciples

MATCH GROUP
a. Ten
b. Twelve
c. Ten with two alternates

2. (200 pts.)
MATCH WORD: Occupations of the disciples

MATCH GROUP
a. One was a tax collector
b. All were fishermen
c. Most were rabbis

3. (300 pts.)
MATCH WORD: Thomas

MATCH GROUP
a. Was also called Thaddaeus
b. Was not an original apostle
c. Doubted Jesus' resurrection

4. (400 pts.)
MATCH WORD: John

MATCH GROUP
a. Spent his final years on Elba
b. Walked on water with Jesus
c. Wrote five books of the Bible

5. (500 pts.)
MATCH WORD: Family relationships among the
disciples

MATCH GROUP
a. One set of brothers
b. One father and son
c. Two sets of brothers

MATCH 'EM

6. (600 pts.)
MATCH WORD: Judas

MATCH GROUP
a. Judas Iscariot was an original apostle
b. Judas son of James betrayed Jesus
c. Judas betrayed Jesus for thirty gold coins

7. (700 pts.)
MATCH WORD: Peter

MATCH GROUP
a. Freed from prison by an angel
b. Exiled to Patmos
c. Had a dream about a ladder to heaven

8. (800 pts.)
MATCH WORD: Deaths of the disciples

MATCH GROUP
a. Peter drowned in the Sea of Galilee
b. James was the first to be martyred
c. John was crucified upside down

9. (900 pts.)

MATCH WORD: Replacement of a disciple

MATCH GROUP

a. Judas was replaced by Stephen
b. Judas was replaced by Matthias
c. Judas was replaced by Barsabbas

10. (1,000 pts.)

MATCH WORD: Names of the disciples

MATCH GROUP

a. James and Thaddaeus were known
as the "Sons of Thunder"
b. Thomas was known as the son of Alphaeus
c. John was known as the son of Zebedee

Quiz 2 Total Points: _____

Cumulative Score: _____

Quiz 3:

Speaking in Parables

1. (100 pts.)
MATCH WORD: The kingdom of heaven

MATCH GROUP
a. Is like a ketchup seed
b. Is like a lost sapphire
c. Is like yeast in dough

2. (200 pts.)
MATCH WORD: The kingdom of heaven

MATCH GROUP
a. Is like a field of flowers
b. Is like a merchant who finds a pearl
c. Is like a fishing boat

3. (300 pts.)
MATCH WORD: The Soils

MATCH GROUP
a. There are five types of soils
b. The rocky soil produced no plants
c. Birds ate some of the seed

4. (400 pts.)
MATCH WORD: The Lost Son

MATCH GROUP
a. The father gave his lost son a ring and sandals
b. The father gave his lost son a chariot and horses
c. The father gave his lost son a vineyard

5. (500 pts.)
MATCH WORD: The Wedding Feast

MATCH GROUP
a. The king's daughter had been married
b. The invited guests refused to come
c. The guest not wearing wedding clothes was seated at
the king's table

MATCH 'EM

6. (600 pts.)

MATCH WORD: The Two Sons

MATCH GROUP

a. The first son did not work in the vineyard

b. The second son worked in the vineyard

c. The first son represents those entering the kingdom of God

7. (700 pts.)

MATCH WORD: The Good Samaritan

MATCH GROUP

a. A man was traveling from Jerusalem to Capernaum

b. The Samaritan gave the innkeeper two silver coins

c. Three religious men passed by the wounded man

8. (800 pts.)

MATCH WORD: The Rich Fool

MATCH GROUP

a. The rich fool wanted to tear down his barns

b. A famine had destroyed the rich fool's crops

c. The rich fool lived to be 108 years old

9. (900 pts.)
MATCH WORD: The Vineyard Workers

MATCH GROUP
a. The last vineyard workers were hired at the eleventh hour
b. The vineyard workers hired first received two denarii
c. The first vineyard workers were hired at the sixth hour

10. (1,000 pts.)
MATCH WORD: The King's Ten Servants

MATCH GROUP
a. The servant who earned five more minas took charge of five vineyards
b. The servant who earned ten more minas took charge of ten cities
c. The king's subjects went into mourning when the king left

Quiz 3 Total Points: _____

Cumulative Score: _____

Quiz 4:

Seeing and Believing

(Jesus' Miracles)

1. (100 pts.)
MATCH WORD: Calming the storm

MATCH GROUP
a. Jesus was piloting the boat
b. Jesus was having a meal
c. Jesus was sleeping

2. (200 pts.)
MATCH WORD: Walking on water

MATCH GROUP
a. The apostles thought Jesus was a ghost
b. Peter sank to the bottom of the lake
c. The apostles still did not believe Jesus
was the Son of God

3. (300 pts.)
MATCH WORD: Healing a paralyzed man

MATCH GROUP
a. The man was brought in through a window
b. Jesus healed him without seeing him
c. The man was lowered through the roof

4. (400 pts.)
MATCH WORD: Lazarus

MATCH GROUP
a. Lived in Capernaum with his two sisters
b. Had been in the tomb for four days
c. Came out of the tomb in his own clothes

5. (500 pts.)
MATCH WORD: Jairus's daughter

MATCH GROUP
a. Jairus was a Roman centurion
b. Jairus's daughter had died
c. Once healed, the girl remained in bed for days

MATCH 'EM

6. (600 pts.)
MATCH WORD: Cana

MATCH GROUP
a. Site of Jesus' last miracle
b. Where Jesus' disciples asked
the servants to fill jars with water
c. Where Mary told Jesus the wine was gone

7. (700 pts.)
MATCH WORD: Healing

MATCH GROUP
a. Jesus healed a Roman centurion's nephew
b. Jesus healed Peter's mother-in-law
c. Jesus healed a Pharisee in his home

8. (800 pts.)
MATCH WORD: Healing on the Sabbath

MATCH GROUP
a. Jesus refused to heal on the Sabbath
b. Jesus healed a demon-possessed man on the Sabbath
c. Jesus healed a man's shriveled hand on the Sabbath

9. (900 pts.)
MATCH WORD: Feeding the 4,000

MATCH GROUP

a. Five loaves and two fish fed the crowd
b. Seven loaves and a few fish fed the crowd
c. Eight basketfuls were left over

10. (1,000 pts.)
MATCH WORD: Feeding the 5,000

MATCH GROUP

a. John the Baptist had recently been beheaded
b. Five loaves and four fish fed the crowd
c. Lazarus had been in his tomb two days

Quiz 4 Total Points: _____

Cumulative Score: _____

Quiz 5:
Mother Lode
Part I

1. (100 pts.)
MATCH WORD: Bathsheba

MATCH GROUP
a. Her first son with David would one day be king
b. David first saw her at the city gate
c. Nathan predicted her son's death

2. (200 pts.)
MATCH WORD: Naomi

MATCH GROUP
a. She lost her husband and two sons in a tragic accident
b. Both of her daughters-in-law were from Moab
c. She was originally from Samaria

3. (300 pts.)
MATCH WORD: Hannah

MATCH GROUP

a. Her husband, Elkanah, had no children
b. Eli the priest thought she was drunk
c. Eli's sons told her to leave the temple

4. (400 pts.)
MATCH WORD: Hannah

MATCH GROUP

a. Samuel means "rock of Israel"
b. Samuel was her only child
c. Samuel means "because I asked the Lord for him"

5. (500 pts.)
MATCH WORD: Naomi

MATCH GROUP

a. She went with Orpah and Ruth to Bethlehem
b. Her grandson was named Obed
c. Boaz was her closest living relative

6. (600 pts.)
MATCH WORD: Elizabeth

MATCH GROUP
a. Mary stayed with her for six months
b. Her husband regained his sight at their son's birth
c. Her husband said their son would be a prophet

7. (700 pts.)
MATCH WORD: Eunice

MATCH GROUP
a. Mother of John Mark
b. Mother of Barnabas
c. Mother of Timothy

8. (800 pts.)
MATCH WORD: Elizabeth

MATCH GROUP
a. She and Zechariah were descendants of Aaron
b. Her husband, Zechariah, was told he would be blind until the birth of his son
c. The angel Gabriel appeared to Zechariah in their home

9. (900 pts.)
MATCH WORD: Eunice

MATCH GROUP
a. Her mother was Rhoda
b. Her mother was Lois
c. Her mother was Lydia

10. (1,000 pts.)
MATCH WORD: Bathsheba

MATCH GROUP
a. Mother of Absalom
b. Mother of Adonijah
c. Mother of Shammua

Quiz 5 Total Points: _____

Cumulative Score: _____

Quiz 6:
Mother Lode
Part II

1. (100 pts.)
MATCH WORD: Hagar

MATCH GROUP
a. She was Abram's first wife
b. She and Sarai were half sisters
c. She ran away from Sarai

2. (200 pts.)
MATCH WORD: Eve

MATCH GROUP
a. She was created from Adam's clavicle
b. She wore clothes made from pomegranate leaves
c. Her sin led to pain in childbirth

3. (300 pts.)
MATCH WORD: Sarah

MATCH GROUP
a. She outlived Abraham by twenty years
b. Isaac means "the first of many children"
c. She gave Hagar to Abraham to be his wife

4. (400 pts.)
MATCH WORD: Mary, earthly mother of Jesus

MATCH GROUP
a. She and Joseph offered a pair of goats
when they presented Jesus at the temple courts
b. She received a blessing from Simeon
c. She received a blessing from the young prophetess Anna

5. (500 pts.)
MATCH WORD: Rebekah

MATCH GROUP
a. Her first son was Esau
b. Her first son was Jacob
c. Jacob sold Esau his birthright

6. (600 pts.)
MATCH WORD: Hagar

MATCH GROUP

a. She was told by an angel her son would live in peace

b. She was told by an angel her descendants would be numerous

c. She was told by an angel her son would be a wild hyena of a man

7. (700 pts.)
MATCH WORD: Eve

MATCH GROUP

a. Her first son was Abel
b. Her first son was Cain
c. Her first son was Seth

8. (800 pts.)
MATCH WORD: Sarah

MATCH GROUP

a. She married her half brother Abraham

b. She gave birth to Isaac when she was seventy

c. She first met Abraham under the great tree of Moreh

9. (900 pts.)
MATCH WORD: Mary, earthly mother of Jesus

MATCH GROUP
a. She could not bear to watch Jesus on the cross
b. She anointed Jesus' head with expensive perfume
c. She went to live with John after the crucifixion

10. (1,000 pts.)
MATCH WORD: Rebekah

MATCH GROUP
a. She was given a nose ring by Abraham's servant
b. Isaac had to work seven years to marry her
c. She wanted Esau to receive Isaac's blessing

Quiz 6 Total Points: _____

Cumulative Score: _____

Quiz 7:

Pater Patter

1. (100 pts.)
MATCH WORD: Joseph

MATCH GROUP
a. He dreamed of a vine with three branches that budded
b. He wore his coat of many colors in Pharaoh's palace
c. He dreamed his brothers bowed down to him

2. (200 pts.)
MATCH WORD: Joseph, husband of Mary

MATCH GROUP
a. He was not a direct descendant of David
b. The seer Simeon told him to flee to Egypt with Jesus
c. He wanted to obtain a divorce from Mary

3. (300 pts.)
MATCH WORD: Jacob

MATCH GROUP

a. At Haran he dreamed of a stairway to heaven
b. He worked seven years to marry Rachel
c. He was the father of twelve children

4. (400 pts.)
MATCH WORD: Job

MATCH GROUP

a. Satan was not allowed to destroy Job's children
b. His wife told him to curse God and die
c. God spoke to him in a still, small voice

5. (500 pts.)
MATCH WORD: Jesse

MATCH GROUP

a. His eldest son was anointed king by Samuel
b. His son David appeared pale and sickly
c. His father was Obed

MATCH 'EM

6. (600 pts.)
MATCH WORD: Terah

MATCH GROUP
a. He was the grandfather of Lot
b. He was the grandfather of Haran
c. He was the grandfather of Nahor

7. (700 pts.)
MATCH WORD: Saul

MATCH GROUP
a. To marry his daughter Michal, David killed 200 Philistines
b. His daughter Merab was one of David's wives
c. His son Jonathan plotted to kill David while he was sleeping

8. (800 pts.)
MATCH WORD: Adam

MATCH GROUP
a. He was created on the fifth day
b. He was created on the first day
c. He was created on the sixth day

9. (900 pts.)

MATCH WORD: Jephthah

MATCH GROUP

a. He asked God to help him triumph over the
   Philistines
b. He made a vow to God that he could not break
c. He sacrificed the eldest of his four children

10. (1,000 pts.)

MATCH WORD: Noah

MATCH GROUP

a. His grandfather was Methuselah
b. His father was Laban
c. From his four sons came the world's people

Quiz 7 Total Points: _____

Cumulative Score: _____

Quiz 8:
Sibling Rivalry

1. (100 pts.)
MATCH WORD: Ishmael and Isaac

MATCH GROUP

a. Isaac and Ishmael were inseparable as children
b. Sarah saw Ishmael mocking Isaac
c. Abraham refused to send Hagar and Ishmael away

2. (200 pts.)
MATCH WORD: Aaron and Moses

MATCH GROUP

a. Aaron had a speech impediment,
so Moses talked to Pharaoh
b. Moses created a golden calf from the Hebrews' gold
c. Aaron's staff became a snake

3. (300 pts.)
MATCH WORD: Joseph and his brothers

MATCH GROUP
a. Joseph had his own silver cup placed in Benjamin's sack
b. Reuben asked to stay in Egypt in place of Benjamin
c. Joseph's brothers sold him for 30 shekels to Midianite merchants

4. (400 pts.)
MATCH WORD: Mary and Martha

MATCH GROUP
a. Martha met Jesus when he arrived after Lazarus's death
b. Mary was known to busy herself with household chores
c. Mary preferred to sit with Jesus rather than to help Martha

5. (500 pts.)
MATCH WORD: Ham, Shem, and Japheth

MATCH GROUP
a. Ham was to be Shem and Japheth's slave
b. Abraham and David are descendants of Japheth
c. Shem was to be Japheth's slave

MATCH 'EM

6. (600 pts.)

MATCH WORD: Cain and Abel

MATCH GROUP

a. Abel worked the soil while Cain tended the sheep

b. Abel was sentenced by God to wander the earth

c. Cain was sent to live east of Eden

7. (700 pts.)

MATCH WORD: Rachel and Leah

MATCH GROUP

a. Rachel had "weak" eyes, but Leah was considered beautiful

b. Rachel gave Jacob her servant to be his wife

c. Leah had two daughters and five sons with Jacob

8. (800 pts.)

MATCH WORD: Jacob and Esau

MATCH GROUP

a. Esau refused to sell Jacob his birthright

b. Esau, with 500 men, once attacked Jacob

c. Jacob once bowed seven times to Esau

9. (900 pts.)
MATCH WORD: Miriam and Moses

MATCH GROUP
a. Miriam rescued Moses from drowning in the Nile
b. Miriam didn't like Moses' Midianite wife
c. Moses asked God to heal Miriam of her leprosy

10. (1,000 pts.)
MATCH WORD: Absalom, Amnon, and Tamar

MATCH GROUP
a. Amnon fell in love with his half sister Tamar
b. Absalom banished Amnon from Israel
c. Absalom killed himself out of shame for his sister

Quiz 8 Total Points: _____

Cumulative Score: _____

Quiz 9:
Splitting Heirs

1. (100 pts.)
MATCH WORD: Ahab

MATCH GROUP
a. His wife, Jezebel, made good on her threat to kill Elijah
b. He had a man murdered for his vineyard
c. He did more good than any king in Israel before him

2. (200 pts.)
MATCH WORD: Jonathan

MATCH GROUP
a. He thrust his sword into his father, Saul,
   as he was dying
b. He warned David to flee by shooting arrows
c. His disabled son, Mephibosheth,
   was refused a place at David's table

3. (300 pts.)
MATCH WORD: Solomon

MATCH GROUP
a. He asked God first for wealth and then for wisdom
b. He finished building the temple started by his father
c. His mother, Bathsheba, feared for her life before he
   was made king

4. (400 pts.)
MATCH WORD: Hezekiah

MATCH GROUP
a. He was the last king of Israel
b. As a sign to him, God made the shadow
   go forward ten steps on a sundial
c. God added fifteen years to his life

5. (500 pts.)
MATCH WORD: Jeroboam

MATCH GROUP
a. He was told by a prophet that he would rule ten
   tribes in Israel
b. Solomon chose him as his successor
c. He built his own shrines at Jerusalem

MATCH 'EM

6. (600 pts.)
MATCH WORD: Rehoboam

MATCH GROUP
a. He followed in David's footsteps
by worshiping the Lord
b. He sold all the treasures of the temple to Jeroboam
c. He ruled over only one tribe

7. (700 pts.)
MATCH WORD: Josiah

MATCH GROUP
a. He was seven years old when he began his reign
b. He destroyed all forms of idol worship except Asherah
poles
c. He renewed Judah's covenant with God

8. (800 pts.)
MATCH WORD: Adonijah

MATCH GROUP
a. He became king without telling his father, David
b. Solomon killed him while he was sleeping
c. He had his future wife's husband killed in battle

41

9. (900 pts.)
MATCH WORD: Asa

MATCH GROUP

a. He erected Asherah poles and set up an altar for Baal
b. He deposed his grandmother for setting up an Asherah pole
c. During his reign there were no wars

10. (1,000 pts.)
MATCH WORD: Joash

MATCH GROUP

a. He was hidden for six years from his grandmother
b. He removed all the high places and idols during his reign
c. He was eight years old when he began his reign

Quiz 9 Total Points: _____

Cumulative Score: _____

Quiz 10:
Who's Who
Part II

1. (100 pts.)
MATCH WORD: Peter

MATCH GROUP
a. Found a coin in a fish's mouth
b. Accompanied Paul on his first missionary journey
c. Was one of seven apostles chosen to distribute food

2. (200 pts.)
MATCH WORD: Sapphira

MATCH GROUP
a. Was brought back to life by Peter
b. Lied to Peter about the sale of property
c. Was a tentmaker in Corinth

3. (300 pts.)
MATCH WORD: (King) Saul

MATCH GROUP
a. Was killed fighting in battle on Mount Gilboa
b. Lost two of his sons in battle on Mount Gilboa
c. Took his own life

4. (400 pts.)
MATCH WORD: Laban

MATCH GROUP
a. Lived in Haran
b. Was a wealthy camel breeder
c. Was Rebekah's cousin

5. (500 pts.)
MATCH WORD: Ananias

MATCH GROUP
a. Took Saul to meet other apostles in Jerusalem
b. Called for Peter to come to his house
c. Placed his hands on Saul

MATCH 'EM

MATCH WORD: Hananiah

MATCH GROUP
a. Nebuchadnezzar's chief official
b. His Babylonian name was Shadrach
c. Prophet to Nineveh

7. (700 pts.)
MATCH WORD: Malchus

MATCH GROUP
a. Last of the minor prophets
b. High priest's servant who lost an ear
c. Replaced Judas Iscariot as one of the apostles

8. (800 pts.)
MATCH WORD: James

MATCH GROUP
a. Was not one of the original apostles
b. Witnessed the Transfiguration
c. With Peter, made preparations for Jesus' last Passover

9. (900 pts.)
MATCH WORD: Ephraim

MATCH GROUP
a. Younger son of Joseph
b. Forefather of Jesus
c. Firstborn son of Joseph

10. (1,000 pts.)
MATCH WORD: Zerubbabel

MATCH GROUP
a. Led the second group of exiles from
Babylon to Jerusalem
b. Rebuilt the temple in Jerusalem
c. Was one of Governor Darius's chief officials

Quiz 10 Total Points: _____

Cumulative Score: _____

Quiz 11:
Waterlogged

1. (100 pts.)
MATCH WORD: Jesus' baptism

MATCH GROUP
a. Occurred in the Sea of Galilee
b. Occurred in the Jordan River
c. Occurred in the Dead Sea

2. (200 pts.)
MATCH WORD: The woman at the well

MATCH GROUP
a. Jesus told her she had four husbands
b. She told Jesus she had a husband
c. She knew Messiah was coming

3. (300 pts.)
MATCH WORD: Water from the rock

MATCH GROUP
a. Aaron struck the rock at Horeb
b. Moses called the place "Meribah" because the people were happy
c. Moses struck the rock at Horeb

4. (400 pts.)
MATCH WORD: Crossing the Jordan

MATCH GROUP
a. The priests carrying the ark of the covenant entered the water first
b. The water was less than a foot deep and placid
c. Moses led the people across the Jordan

5. (500 pts.)
MATCH WORD: The Flood

MATCH GROUP
a. Noah was 500 years old when the flood came
b. Noah took seven pairs of every clean animal onto the ark
c. The waters flooded the earth for fifty days

MATCH 'EM

6. (600 pts.)

MATCH WORD: The plague of blood

MATCH GROUP

a. Egypt's magicians were unable to change water into blood

b. Aaron struck the Nile with his staff

c. Despite the plague, Egyptians could still drink the water

7. (700 pts.)

MATCH WORD: Pool of Siloam

MATCH GROUP

a. Where Jesus sent a blind man

b. Where Jesus sent a demon-possessed man

c. Where Jesus sent a woman who was bleeding

8. (800 pts.)

MATCH WORD: Crossing the Red Sea

MATCH GROUP

a. God led the Hebrews by the desert road to the Red Sea

b. Aaron carried the bones of Joseph across the Red Sea

c. Aaron stretched out his hand over the Red Sea

9. (900 pts.)
MATCH WORD: Creation

MATCH GROUP
a. On the fourth day God filled the water with fish
b. On the third day God created sky as separate from water
c. On the third day God called the waters "seas"

10. (1,000 pts.)
MATCH WORD: Paul's shipwreck

MATCH GROUP
a. Occurred in the Mediterranean Sea
b. Occurred in the Ionian Sea
c. Occurred in the Adriatic Sea

Quiz 11 Total Points: _____

Cumulative Score: _____

Quiz 12:
Angelic Chorus

1. (100 pts.)
MATCH WORD: Mary, earthly mother of Jesus

MATCH GROUP
a. Gabriel visited Mary in Bethlehem
b. Gabriel told Mary that Elizabeth was pregnant
c. Mary told the angel she would have no part of this plan

2. (200 pts.)
MATCH WORD: Shepherds

MATCH GROUP
a. A great host of angels first greeted the shepherds
b. Upon seeing the angel, the shepherds
went immediately to Bethlehem
c. The shepherds kept the news of the
angels to themselves

3. (300 pts.)
MATCH WORD: Zechariah

MATCH GROUP
a. Was told by the angel to name his son John
b. The angel's name was Michael
c. The angel appeared at his home in Jerusalem

4. (400 pts.)
MATCH WORD: Hagar

MATCH GROUP
a. An angel told her to name her son Ishmael
b. An angel appeared to her on Mount Horeb
c. An angel appeared to her in Sarai's tent

5. (500 pts.)
MATCH WORD: The women at the tomb

MATCH GROUP
a. The angel was sitting on the stone in front of Jesus' tomb
b. The angel did not speak to the women
c. The angel was sitting inside the tomb

6. (600 pts.)
MATCH WORD: Paul

MATCH GROUP
a. An angel told him he would not stand trial in Rome
b. An angel told him only two lives
would be lost in a shipwreck
c. An angel told him all on board ship would be saved

7. (700 pts.)
MATCH WORD: Lot

MATCH GROUP
a. The angels wanted to spend the night at Lot's house
b. Lot's sons-in-law invited the angels to their houses
c. The angels blinded the men of Sodom

8. (800 pts.)
MATCH WORD: Balaam

MATCH GROUP
a. He beat his donkey three times,
whenever the angel appeared
b. The angel told him to say anything to Balak
c. The angel broke his arm

9. (900 pts.)
MATCH WORD: Daniel

MATCH GROUP

a. Daniel's companions also saw the angel
b. The angel appeared to Daniel at Cyrus's palace
c. The angel came to tell Daniel what is written in the Book of Truth

10. (1,000 pts.)
MATCH WORD: Revelation

MATCH GROUP

a. The seven lampstands are the seven angels
b. John was to write to the angels of seven churches
c. The seven angels brought John food on Patmos

Quiz 12 Total Points: _____

Cumulative Score: _____

Quiz 13:
Where There's Smoke. . .

1. (100 pts.)

MATCH WORD: Burning bush

MATCH GROUP

a. God asked Moses to remove his tunic
b. Was on Mount Horeb
c. After the bushed burned up, God spoke to Moses

2. (200 pts.)

MATCH WORD: Worship of Baal

MATCH GROUP

a. Elijah's fire consumed even the stones and the soil
b. The prophets of Baal stopped shouting at midday
c. The prophets of Baal got a little fire going, but then it went out

3. (300 pts.)
MATCH WORD: Pillar of fire

MATCH GROUP
a. Covered the tabernacle at night
b. At this sign, the Israelites set out on their journey
c. At this sign, the Israelites made camp

4. (400 pts.)
MATCH WORD: Fiery furnace

MATCH GROUP
a. Shadrach, Meshach, and Abednego wore only trousers in the furnace
b. King Nebuchadnezzar ordered the furnace seven times hotter
c. King Nebuchadnezzar saw five men inside the furnace

5. (500 pts.)
MATCH WORD: Ten Commandments

MATCH GROUP
a. Mount Carmel was covered with smoke
b. Moses got lost going up the mountain because of all the smoke
c. Mount Sinai was covered with smoke

MATCH 'EM

6. (600 pts.)
MATCH WORD: Tongues of fire

MATCH GROUP
a. In Bethany on the day of Pentecost
b. Rested only on the twelve apostles
c. Habakkuk had foretold this event

7. (700 pts.)
MATCH WORD: Chariot of fire

MATCH GROUP
a. Elijah was taken up to heaven by the Sea of Galilee
b. Elijah left his cloak behind after departing in the chariot
c. Elisha was taken up into heaven in the chariot

8. (800 pts.)
MATCH WORD: Burnt offerings

MATCH GROUP
a. Didn't need to burn all night
b. Priests were to wear woolen garments when presenting them
c. The priests were to burn the fat of the offering first

9. (900 pts.)
MATCH WORD: Satan's destruction

MATCH GROUP
a. By another flood
b. By fire, before the 1,000-year period of peace
c. By fire, after the 1,000-year period of peace

10. (1,000 pts.)
MATCH WORD: Nadab and Abihu

MATCH GROUP
a. Sons of Aaron who put fire in their censers
b. Sons of Moses who offered burnt offerings
c. Sons of Miriam who could swallow fire

Quiz 13 Total Points: _____

Cumulative Score: _____

Quiz 14:
Notable Numbers

1. (100 pts.)
MATCH WORD: Twelve

MATCH GROUP

a. Age of Jesus when he stayed behind in the temple in Jerusalem
b. Days spent by Mary and Joseph looking for Jesus in Jerusalem
c. Loaves and fish needed to feed 5,000

2. (200 pts.)
MATCH WORD: Forty

MATCH GROUP

a. Height in feet of Noah's ark
b. Days Jesus was tempted by Satan in the desert
c. Age of David when he became king of Israel and Judah

3. (300 pts.)
MATCH WORD: Twelve

MATCH GROUP

a. Stones from Jordan used to make a monument
b. Sons of Jesse
c. Hour of the day when Jesus died

4. (400 pts.)
MATCH WORD: Forty

MATCH GROUP

a. Times the Israelites marched around Jericho
b. Days the spies spent exploring Canaan
c. Age of Saul when he became king

5. (500 pts.)
MATCH WORD: Seven

MATCH GROUP

a. Lost tribes of Israel
b. Churches Jesus tells John to write
c. Fruits of the spirit

MATCH 'EM

6. (600 pts.)
MATCH WORD: Three

MATCH GROUP

a. Shelters Peter wanted to erect at the Transfiguration
b. Coins given by poor widow to temple treasury
c. Criminals crucified with Jesus

7. (700 pts.)
MATCH WORD: Three

MATCH GROUP

a. Additional apostles chosen to distribute food
b. Dreams Pilate's wife had before Jesus' sentencing
c. Days Saul (Paul) was blind in Damascus

8. (800 pts.)
MATCH WORD: Two

MATCH GROUP

a. Days Jonah was inside the great fish
b. Arrows Jonathan shot into
the woods as a sign to David
c. Wives of Elkanah

9. (900 pts.)
MATCH WORD: Seventy

MATCH GROUP

a. Believers who were baptized after Pentecost
b. Elders of Israel appointed by Moses
c. Elders surrounding the throne of God in heaven

10. (1,000 pts.)
MATCH WORD: One (First)

MATCH GROUP

a. Month of Hebrew calendar when
Purim was celebrated
b. Month of Hebrew calendar when
the Feast of Trumpets was celebrated
c. Month of Hebrew calendar when
Passover was celebrated

Quiz 14 Total Points: _____

Cumulative Score: _____

Quiz 15:
Climb Every One

1. (100 pts.)
MATCH WORD: Ararat

MATCH GROUP
a. Where Moses received the Ten Commandments
b. Where Moses struck the rock and water burst out
c. Where Noah's ark came to rest

2. (200 pts.)
MATCH WORD: Sinai (Horeb)

MATCH GROUP
a. Where the Israelites joined Moses
at the top to see God
b. Where Aaron was asked by God to join Moses
c. Where Moses was speechless and said nothing to God

3. (300 pts.)
MATCH WORD: Olivet (Olives)

MATCH GROUP

a. Where Jesus walked with two men after His resurrection
b. Where Jesus told His disciples signs of the end times
c. Where Jesus turned water into wine

4. (400 pts.)
MATCH WORD: Carmel

MATCH GROUP

a. Where Elijah ascended on a chariot of fire
b. Where Ahab assembled the prophets of Baal
c. Where Elijah hid from Jezebel

5. (500 pts.)
MATCH WORD: Horeb (Sinai)

MATCH GROUP

a. Where God appeared to Elisha in a whisper
b. Where God appeared to King Ahab in an earthquake
c. Where God appeared to Elijah in a whisper

MATCH 'EM

6. (600 pts.)
MATCH WORD: Olivet (Olives)

MATCH GROUP
a. Where David fled to escape Adonijah
b. Where David fled to escape Saul
c. Where David fled to escape Absalom

7. (700 pts.)
MATCH WORD: Tabor

MATCH GROUP
a. Where Saul was told by Samuel he would meet three men
b. Where Saul was told by Samuel he would meet two men
c. Where Saul was anointed king by Samuel

8. (800 pts.)
MATCH WORD: Carmel

MATCH GROUP
a. Where the Shunammite woman found Elisha
b. Where the Shunammite woman found Elijah
c. Where Elisha received a double portion of Elijah's spirit

9. (900 pts.)
MATCH WORD: Tabor

MATCH GROUP
a. Where Sisera met Jael
b. Where Barak descended to meet Sisera
c. Where Barak found the dead Sisera

10. (1,000 pts.)
MATCH WORD: Hermon

MATCH GROUP
a. Northernmost boundary of land conquered
by Joshua east of the Jordan
b. Southernmost boundary of land conquered
by Joshua east of the Jordan
c. Northernmost boundary of land conquered
by Joshua west of the Jordan

Quiz 15 Total Points: _____

Cumulative Score: _____

Quiz 16:
Power in the Name

1. (100 pts.)

MATCH WORD: How Jesus became the Nazarene

MATCH GROUP

a. Joseph was told to go to Nazareth in a dream
b. Simeon told Joseph to go to Nazareth
c. Zechariah told Joseph to go to Nazareth

2. (200 pts.)

MATCH WORD: Wonderful Counselor

MATCH GROUP

a. First used by Jeremiah
b. First used by Isaiah
c. First used in the Psalms by David

3. (300 pts.)
MATCH WORD: Why Jesus was the Son of God

MATCH GROUP

a. A bleeding woman was healed by touching Jesus' arm
b. A bleeding woman was healed by touching Jesus' hand
c. A bleeding woman was healed by touching Jesus' cloak

4. (400 pts.)
MATCH WORD: How Jesus as Redeemer will return

MATCH GROUP

a. Jesus will come again in the clouds
b. An earthquake will announce Jesus' second coming
c. Jesus will come amid loud claps of
thunder and lightning

5. (500 pts.)
MATCH WORD: A sign Jesus is the Prince of Peace

MATCH GROUP

a. A lamb without blemish was at Jesus' baptism
b. A dove alit on Jesus after His baptism
c. A rainbow appeared overhead after Jesus' baptism

6. (600 pts.)

MATCH WORD: Good Shepherd

MATCH GROUP

a. Baby Jesus was greeted first by shepherds

b. Jesus was raised by Joseph, a shepherd

c. Many of Jesus' disciples were shepherds

7. (700 pts.)

MATCH WORD: Lamb of God

MATCH GROUP

a. Jesus did not celebrate Passover the year He was crucified

b. Only Jesus as the Lamb was worthy to open the seven seals

c. Jesus was crucified by Himself

8. (800 pts.)

MATCH WORD: Everlasting Father

MATCH GROUP

a. Jesus waited four days to heal a widow's son

b. Jesus went to the tombs in Nain to heal a widow's son

c. Jesus touched the coffin in a funeral procession and healed a widow's son

9. (900 pts.)
MATCH WORD: High Priest

MATCH GROUP

a. Jesus was descended from the high priest Nadab
b. Jesus was descended from the tribe of Levi
c. Jesus is a high priest of the order of Melchizedek

10. (1,000 pts.)
MATCH WORD: Branch

MATCH GROUP

a. So named by Isaiah
b. So named by Jeremiah
c. So named by Daniel

Quiz 16 Total Points: _____

Cumulative Score: _____

Quiz 17:
You Say Elijah. . .

1. (100 pts.)
MATCH WORD: Floating axhead

MATCH GROUP
a. To retrieve it, Elisha threw a stick in the Jordan
b. To retrieve it, Gehazi jumped in the Jordan and drowned
c. To retrieve it, Elijah threw his cloak in the water

2. (200 pts.)
MATCH WORD: Widow at Zarephath

MATCH GROUP
a. Elisha told her she would have food until the rains came
b. Elisha asked her for a piece of bread
c. Elijah prayed for her son's life

3. (300 pts.)

MATCH WORD: How Ahab acquired Naboth's vineyard

MATCH GROUP

a. As a result, Elijah said every descendant of Ahab would be killed
b. As a result, Elisha said only Jezebel would be spared
c. Elijah brought Naboth back to life

4. (400 pts.)

MATCH WORD: Naaman

MATCH GROUP

a. Was told by Elisha to wash in the Jordan
b. Wrote to Elisha asking him to cure him
c. Washed himself in the rivers of Damascus

5. (500 pts.)

MATCH WORD: Elisha

MATCH GROUP

a. Told the kings of Israel and Judah to bring him a lute player
b. Told a widow to ask her neighbors for empty jars
c. Told a Shunammite woman she would be barren

6. (600 pts.)
MATCH WORD: Obadiah

MATCH GROUP
a. Led Jezebel to find Elijah
b. Refused Elisha's demand that he tell Ahab
he had found the prophet
c. Was in charge of Ahab's palace

7. (700 pts.)
MATCH WORD: Elijah

MATCH GROUP
a. Known as "the Hittite"
b. Known as "the Tishbite"
c. Known as "the Merarite"

8. (800 pts.)
MATCH WORD: Gehazi

MATCH GROUP
a. Asked Naaman for two talents of silver
b. Lied to Elisha and became leprous
c. Asked Elijah for a cake of bread

9. (900 pts.)
MATCH WORD: King Jehoash

MATCH GROUP

a. Was told by Elisha to strike the ground with his arrows
b. Upon Elisha's instruction, struck the ground five times with his arrows
c. Was told by Elijah to strike the ground three times

10. (1,000 pts.)
MATCH WORD: Hazael

MATCH GROUP

a. Was told by Elisha that he would die
b. Was told by Elisha that he would be king of Judah
c. Asked Elisha if the king of Aram would get well

Quiz 17 Total Points: _____

Cumulative Score: _____

Quiz 18:
People of the Cloth

1. (100 pts.)
MATCH WORD: Jesus

MATCH GROUP
a. Upon birth, wrapped in purple cloth by Mary
b. Upon birth, encompassed in Joseph's robes
c. Upon birth, wrapped in bands of cloth by Mary

2. (200 pts.)
MATCH WORD: Adam and Eve

MATCH GROUP
a. Adam made garments for Eve and himself
b. God made garments for them
c. Eve made garments out of animal skins

3. (300 pts.)
MATCH WORD: John the Baptist

MATCH GROUP

a. Was given hand-me-downs from Zechariah
b. Wore camel's hair clothing
c. Wore a coat of foxes' fur

4. (400 pts.)
MATCH WORD: Jesus

MATCH GROUP

a. After His crucifixion, His clothes were
given back to Mary
b. Peter asked the soldiers for Jesus' clothes
c. Wore a seamless undergarment

5. (500 pts.)
MATCH WORD: Rahab

MATCH GROUP

a. Wore a scarlet cord around her neck
b. Wrapped a scarlet cord around her waist
c. Tied a scarlet cord in her window

6. (600 pts.)
MATCH WORD: Lydia

MATCH GROUP
a. Proprietor of fine linen
b. Dealer in purple cloth
c. Known for her camel's hair coats

7. (700 pts.)
MATCH WORD: Hannah

MATCH GROUP
a. Made robes each year for Samuel
b. Made robes each year for Eli and his sons
c. Was known for her fine embroidery

8. (800 pts.)
MATCH WORD: Dorcas

MATCH GROUP
a. Dealer in purple cloth
b. Known for her handmade robes
c. Made robes for Peter

9. (900 pts.)
MATCH WORD: Saul (Paul)

MATCH GROUP
a. Was surrounded by the clothes of witnesses to
   Stephen's stoning
b. Took off his cloak to throw rocks himself
c. Took Stephen's cloak to be his own

10. (1,000 pts.)
MATCH WORD: Jacob

MATCH GROUP
a. Wore Esau's best clothes with goatskin
   on his arms and neck
b. Wore Esau's poorest garments with goatskin
   on his arms and neck
c. Wore his own clothes and goatskin
   on his arms and neck

Quiz 18 Total Points: _____

Cumulative Score: _____

Quiz 19:

Prophets in a Minor Key

1. (100 pts.)
MATCH WORD: Jonah

MATCH GROUP
a. Was on his way to Nineveh when a storm arose
b. Proclaimed that Nineveh would be overturned in seven days
c. When he was thrown overboard, the sea became calm

2. (200 pts.)
MATCH WORD: Micah

MATCH GROUP
a. Son of Tekoa
b. Is the shortest book of the minor prophets
c. Tells of a ruler to come from Bethlehem

3. (300 pts.)
MATCH WORD: Hosea

MATCH GROUP
a. Was sent by God to Nineveh
b. Was told by God to sit under a fig tree
c. Was told by God to marry an adulterous wife

4. (400 pts.)
MATCH WORD: Malachi

MATCH GROUP
a. After him, no prophet would speak
God's voice for 500 years
b. Wrote of the prophet Elijah's return
c. Wrote encouraging the rebuilding of the temple

5. (500 pts.)
MATCH WORD: Amos

MATCH GROUP
a. Was shown a plumb line by God
b. Was shown a bowl of spoiled fruit by God
c. Son of a priest

MATCH 'EM

6. (600 pts.)
MATCH WORD: Haggai

MATCH GROUP
a. His book is addressed to Darius, governor of Babylon
b. Son of Tekoa
c. Wrote of the laying of the temple's cornerstone

7. (700 pts.)
MATCH WORD: Nahum

MATCH GROUP
a. Predicted Babylon's doom
b. Predicted Nineveh's destruction
c. Predicted fifty more prosperous years for Nineveh

8. (800 pts.)
MATCH WORD: Obadiah

MATCH GROUP
a. Preached to the Israelites in Babylon
b. Preached to the Edomites
c. Is the longest book of the minor prophets

9. (900 pts.)
MATCH WORD: Zephaniah

MATCH GROUP
a. Wrote during the reign of King Josiah
b. Son of Pethuel
c. Wrote during the reign of King Uzziah

10. (1,000 pts.)
MATCH WORD: Joel

MATCH GROUP
a. Son of Pethuel
b. Son of Tekoa
c. Son of Obadiah

Quiz 19 Total Points: _____

Cumulative Score: _____

Quiz 20:
Who's Who
Part III

1. (100 pts.)
MATCH WORD: Reuben

MATCH GROUP
a. Brother of Daniel
b. Brother of Judah
c. Brother of Obadiah

2. (200 pts.)
MATCH WORD: Nehemiah

MATCH GROUP
a. Led the first return of exiles to Jerusalem
b. Rebuilt Jerusalem's city walls
c. Led the opposition to building Jerusalem's city walls

3. (300 pts.)
MATCH WORD: Philip

MATCH GROUP

a. One of the original apostles
b. Had four unmarried sons who were evangelists
c. Baptized an Ethiopian eunuch

4. (400 pts.)
MATCH WORD: Herodias

MATCH GROUP

a. Was married to Herod
b. Her daughter danced on Herod's birthday
c. Was married to Herod Antipas

5. (500 pts.)
MATCH WORD: Nicodemus

MATCH GROUP

a. Helped Joseph of Arimathea bury Jesus
b. Went to see Jesus in the afternoon
c. Was a Pharisee who helped condemn Jesus

MATCH 'EM

6. (600 pts.)
MATCH WORD: Achan

MATCH GROUP
a. Father of Othniel, who married Acsah
b. Hid plunder from battles in his tent
c. Was exiled to Babylon

7. (700 pts.)
MATCH WORD: Deborah

MATCH GROUP
a. Wife of Barak
b. Held court under the Palm of Deborah
c. Sister of Jael, Sisera's slayer

8. (800 pts.)
MATCH WORD: Annas

MATCH GROUP
a. Blessed baby Jesus in the temple
b. Father-in-law of Caiaphas
c. Accompanied Paul on his second missionary journey

9. (900 pts.)
MATCH WORD: Eliphaz the Temanite

MATCH GROUP
a. Minor prophet to Israel
b. Friend of Daniel
c. Friend of Job

10. (1,000 pts.)
MATCH WORD: John Mark

MATCH GROUP
a. Went on Paul's first missionary journey
b. Went on Paul's second missionary journey
c. Went on Silas's second missionary journey

Quiz 20 Total Points: _____

Cumulative Score: _____

Quiz 21:
Table for Two

1. (100 pts.)
MATCH WORD: Aquila and Priscilla

MATCH GROUP
a. Sold idols in Ephesus
b. Dealt in fine linen and wool
c. Were tentmakers

2. (200 pts.)
MATCH WORD: David and Bathsheba

MATCH GROUP
a. She was engaged to Uriah when she met David
b. Uriah died the day after Bathsheba
told him of her pregnancy
c. David arranged for Uriah to be put in the front lines

3. (300 pts.)
MATCH WORD: David and Abigail

MATCH GROUP
a. She thought her first husband was a fool
b. Her first husband was one of David's mighty men
c. Her first husband killed himself when she left him for David

4. (400 pts.)
MATCH WORD: Rebekah and Isaac

MATCH GROUP
a. Isaac was comforted by her after Sarah's death
b. She gave water to Abraham's servant but refused to water his camels
c. She refused to leave her family for ten days

5. (500 pts.)
MATCH WORD: Jacob and Rachel

MATCH GROUP
a. She secretly stole her father's idols
b. He worked twenty years to marry Rachel and Leah
c. He thought Laban had treated him fairly

MATCH 'EM

6. (600 pts.)
MATCH WORD: Abraham and Sarah

MATCH GROUP
a. Because of her, Abimelech's family contracted leprosy

b. On two occasions, Abraham called Sarah his sister

c. Abraham and Sarah were first cousins

7. (700 pts.)
MATCH WORD: Samson and Delilah

MATCH GROUP
a. He told her his strength was in his legs

b. Three times he made a fool of her

c. She was paid by the rulers of the Danites

8. (800 pts.)
MATCH WORD: David and Michal

MATCH GROUP
a. She laughed when she saw David dancing

b. David would be her only husband

c. She died childless

9. (900 pts.)
MATCH WORD: Ruth and Boaz

MATCH GROUP

a. Boaz was Ruth's father's cousin
b. Boaz traced his ancestry back to Perez
c. Ruth's father owned some property in Bethlehem

10. (1,000 pts.)
MATCH WORD: Acsah and Othniel

MATCH GROUP

a. Acsah was Joshua's daughter
b. Othniel defeated the Canaanites
at Gaza for Acsah's hand
c. Acsah was Caleb's daughter

Quiz 21 Total Points: _____

Cumulative Score: _____

Quiz 22:
Not Counting Sheep

1. (100 pts.)
MATCH WORD: Joseph, husband of Mary

MATCH GROUP
a. Was told in a dream Herod would kill Jesus
b. Was told in a dream to stay in Egypt three months
c. Was told in a dream to return to Bethlehem

2. (200 pts.)
MATCH WORD: The Magi

MATCH GROUP
a. Were told in a dream to return to Jerusalem
b. Were told in a dream to find John the Baptist
c. Were told in a dream not to return to Herod

3. (300 pts.)
MATCH WORD: Jacob

MATCH GROUP

a. Dreamed of a ladder to heaven
b. Bethel, where he built an altar, means "house of dreams"
c. Returned home to Isaac after having his first dream

4. (400 pts.)
MATCH WORD: Joseph

MATCH GROUP

a. Was sent back to the dungeon after
Pharaoh heard his interpretation of dream
b. Was made third in command in Egypt
after he told Pharaoh his dream
c. Said that the seven good heads of grain
and seven fat cows meant the same thing

5. (500 pts.)
MATCH WORD: Joseph

MATCH GROUP

a. Predicted that the chief baker would be hanged
b. Predicted that the chief cupbearer would be hanged
c. The chief cupbearer never forgot him

MATCH 'EM

6. (600 pts.)
MATCH WORD: Peter

MATCH GROUP
a. Was told in a dream to "kill and eat"
b. Saw a sheet filled with only reptiles
c. Went into a trance at Cornelius's house

7. (700 pts.)
MATCH WORD: Nebuchadnezzar's dream of a statue

MATCH GROUP
a. None of his magicians could interpret his dream
b. He asked his magicians to tell him his dream
c. He put his magicians to death

8. (800 pts.)
MATCH WORD: Nebuchadnezzar's dream of a statue

MATCH GROUP
a. Daniel said a rock was cut out of the statue
b. Daniel said the statue's feet were entirely made of clay
c. The rock that was cut out sank into the ocean

9. (900 pts.)

MATCH WORD: Nebuchadnezzar's dream of a tree

MATCH GROUP

a. The king's magicians interpreted the dream
b. The king repented and avoided fulfillment of the dream
c. Daniel said that the king was the tree

10. (1,000 pts.)

MATCH WORD: Daniel

MATCH GROUP

a. Wrestled with God in a dream
b. Had a dream of four beasts
c. Was told in a dream to rebuild Jerusalem's walls

Quiz 22 Total Points: _____

Cumulative Score: _____

Quiz 23:
Also Known As
Part I

1. (100 pts.)
MATCH WORD: Abraham

MATCH GROUP
a. Melchizedek
b. Abimelech
c. Abram

2. (200 pts.)
MATCH WORD: Sarah

MATCH GROUP
a. Shammah
b. Zerah
c. Sarai

3. (300 pts.)
MATCH WORD: Paul

MATCH GROUP
a. Saul
b. Simon
c. Peter

4. (400 pts.)
MATCH WORD: Peter

MATCH GROUP
a. Simeon
b. Andrew
c. Simon

5. (500 pts.)
MATCH WORD: Esau

MATCH GROUP
a. Edom
b. Eliphaz
c. Ebal

6. (600 pts.)
MATCH WORD: Jacob

MATCH GROUP
a. Judah
b. Israel
c. Ishmael

7. (700 pts.)
MATCH WORD: Meshach

MATCH GROUP
a. Michal
b. Mishael
c. Hananiah

8. (800 pts.)
MATCH WORD: Daniel

MATCH GROUP
a. Belshazzar
b. Belteshazzar
c. Darius

9. (900 pts.)
MATCH WORD: Abednego

MATCH GROUP
a. Azariah
b. Hezekiah
c. Asa

10. (1,000 pts.)
MATCH WORD: Pashhur

MATCH GROUP
a. Magor-Missabib
b. Topheth
c. Zedekiah

Quiz 23 Total Points: _____

Cumulative Score: _____

Quiz 24:
Food for Thought

1. (100 pts.)
MATCH WORD: Fattened calf

MATCH GROUP
a. Parable of the Lost Son
b. Parable of the Soils
c. Parable of the King's Ten Servants

2. (200 pts.)
MATCH WORD: Venison

MATCH GROUP
a. Daniel's diet for seven days
b. One of Isaac's favorite dishes
c. What manna tasted like

3. (300 pts.)
MATCH WORD: Lentil stew

MATCH GROUP
a. Served in the Parable of the Lost Son
b. Served at the wedding in Cana
c. What Jacob made Esau

4. (400 pts.)
MATCH WORD: Grapes

MATCH GROUP
a. What Jael served to Sisera
b. Produce carried back from Canaan by Israel's spies
c. What Ahab choked on

5. (500 pts.)
MATCH WORD: Fish

MATCH GROUP
a. What Jesus served some disciples for breakfast
b. Created on the fourth day
c. Created on the third day

MATCH 'EM

6. (600 pts.)
MATCH WORD: Vegetables

MATCH GROUP
a. Daniel's diet for ten days
b. Esther's beauty secret
c. What Ruth picked in Boaz's fields

7. (700 pts.)
MATCH WORD: Corn (KJV)

MATCH GROUP
a. What the Israelites ate with manna
b. What Shadrach, Meshach, and Abednego ate for
   ten days
c. What the Israelites ate after Passover

8. (800 pts.)
MATCH WORD: Figs

MATCH GROUP
a. What Naboth grew in his orchard
b. What God showed Jeremiah in two baskets
c. What Eve gave to Adam

9. (900 pts.)
MATCH WORD: Figs

MATCH GROUP

a. What Lydia sold in the market in Thyatira
b. What was given to Sennacherib as a poultice
c. What Isaiah put on Hezekiah as a poultice

10. (1,000 pts.)
MATCH WORD: Mandrake plants

MATCH GROUP

a. Jacob's favorite food
b. What Leah gave Rachel in return for Jacob
c. Used to make unleavened bread

Quiz 24 Total Points: _____

Cumulative Score: _____

Quiz 25:
The (Same) Name Game
Part I

1. (100 pts.)
MATCH WORD: Saul

MATCH GROUP
a. Of Tarsus
b. Of Tekoa
c. The Tishbite

2. (200 pts.)
MATCH WORD: Uriah

MATCH GROUP
a. Married to Bathsheba
b. Engaged to Bathsheba
c. Married to Maacah

3. (300 pts.)
MATCH WORD: Joseph

MATCH GROUP
a. Fourth son of Jacob
b. Eldest son of Jacob
c. Potiphar's attendant

4. (400 pts.)
MATCH WORD: Mary

MATCH GROUP
a. Sister of Lazarus
b. Mother of Apollos
c. Daughter of Saul

5. (500 pts.)
MATCH WORD: Mary

MATCH GROUP
a. Sister of Lazarus who busied herself with household
   preparations
b. At the tomb, called Jesus "Rabboni"
c. Mother of John the Baptist

6. (600 pts.)
MATCH WORD: Joseph

MATCH GROUP
a. Member of the Jewish Council
b. Centurion who declared that Jesus was dead
c. Pharisee who vehemently opposed Jesus

7. (700 pts.)
MATCH WORD: Hananiah

MATCH GROUP
a. Also known as Meshach
b. Servant of Elijah
c. Thrown into a fiery furnace

8. (800 pts.)
MATCH WORD: Saul

MATCH GROUP
a. Son of Abiah
b. Son of Abiel
c. Son of Kish

9. (900 pts.)
MATCH WORD: Uriah

MATCH GROUP
a. Chief official of King Zedekiah
b. Prophet killed by King Jehoiakim
c. One of Nebuchadnezzar's sorcerers

10. (1,000 pts.)
MATCH WORD: Hananiah

MATCH GROUP
a. Minor prophet
b. False prophet during Jeremiah's time
c. Seer who greeted baby Jesus

Quiz 25 Total Points: _____

Cumulative Score: _____

Quiz 26:
Notable Numbers
Part I

1. (100 pts.)
MATCH WORD: Twelve

MATCH GROUP
a. Spies sent to Canaan
b. Banquets arranged by Esther for Xerxes and Haman
c. Amorite kings who opposed Joshua at Gibeon

2. (200 pts.)
MATCH WORD: Seventy

MATCH GROUP
a. Number of David's mighty men
b. Years of Babylonian captivity
c. Years Ehud was judge of Israel

3. (300 pts.)
MATCH WORD: One hundred fifty-three

MATCH GROUP
a. Prophets of Baal who opposed Elijah
b. Number of fish once caught by seven disciples
c. Age of Sarah when she died

4. (400 pts.)
MATCH WORD: Three hundred

MATCH GROUP
a. Years between Malachi's prophecy
and the birth of Christ
b. Number of Gideon's men who knelt
down to drink water
c. Number of Gideon's men who
lapped water from their hands

5. (500 pts.)
MATCH WORD: Fourteen

MATCH GROUP
a. Years Samson was judge of Israel
b. Number of original children of Job
c. Generations from Abraham to David

MATCH 'EM

6. (600 pts.)
MATCH WORD: Nine hundred fifty

MATCH GROUP
a. Age of Noah at his death
b. Age of Methuselah at his death
c. Age of Lamech at his death

7. (700 pts.)
MATCH WORD: One hundred

MATCH GROUP
a. In talents, what Sheba gave Solomon in gold
b. In silver pieces, what Jacob paid for land in Canaan
c. People killed by Samson at Lehi

8. (800 pts.)
MATCH WORD: Fourteen

MATCH GROUP
a. Generations from Babylonian exile to birth of Jesus
b. Days Jesus was tempted by Satan in the desert
c. Months Paul spent on Malta

9. (900 pts.)
MATCH WORD: Seventy

MATCH GROUP
a. Number of Solomon's wives
b. Number of half brothers of Abimelech
c. Number of Solomon's concubines

10. (1,000 pts.)
MATCH WORD: Seventeen

MATCH GROUP
a. Years Samson was judge of Israel
b. Shekels of silver paid to Judas for his betrayal
c. Shekels of silver paid by Jeremiah for a field

Quiz 26 Total Points: _____

Cumulative Score: _____

Quiz 27:
How Green Was My. . .

1. (100 pts.)
MATCH WORD: Valley of Kidron

MATCH GROUP
a. Where Jesus gave the Beatitudes
b. Where Jesus brought Lazarus back from the dead
c. Near where Jesus was arrested

2. (200 pts.)
MATCH WORD: Valley of Ben Hinnom

MATCH GROUP
a. Also known as Valley of Hope
b. Also known as Topheth
c. Also known as Valley of Despair

3. (300 pts.)
MATCH WORD: Valley of Elah

MATCH GROUP
a. Where Saul's army camped to meet Goliath
b. Where Solomon was made king
c. Where Satan tempted Jesus

4. (400 pts.)
MATCH WORD: Valley of Jezreel

MATCH GROUP
a. Where David was anointed by Samuel
b. Where Hannah dedicated Samuel to the Lord
c. Where opposing armies were camped to meet Gideon

5. (500 pts.)
MATCH WORD: Valley of Sorek

MATCH GROUP
a. Where Samuel anointed David
b. Where Samson fell in love with Delilah
c. Where Ruth fell in love with Boaz

MATCH 'EM

6. (600 pts.)

MATCH WORD: Valley of Kidron

MATCH GROUP
a. Where David became king of all Israel
b. Where David marched after Absalom became king
c. Where David defeated the Philistines

7. (700 pts.)

MATCH WORD: Valley of Ben Hinnom

MATCH GROUP
a. Where Nebuchadnezzar captured Zedekiah
b. Where human sacrifices were made to Molech
c. Where the Israelites defeated Sihon

8. (800 pts.)

MATCH WORD: Zered Valley

MATCH GROUP
a. Where Moses led the Israelites after
thirty-eight years of wandering
b. Where the Israelites defeated the Moabites
c. Where the Israelites defeated the Ammonites

9. (900 pts.)
MATCH WORD: Valley of Ben Hinnom

MATCH GROUP
a. Where Jeremiah was beaten and put into stocks
b. Where Jeremiah went to live after he was freed by a Babylonian officer
c. Where Jeremiah said to break a potter's jar

10. (1,000 pts.)
MATCH WORD: Valley of Rephaim

MATCH GROUP
a. Where Abner was murdered
b. Where David twice attacked the Philistines
c. Where Saul died after battling the Philistines

Quiz 27 Total Points: _____

Cumulative Score: _____

Quiz 28:
Hold fast

1. (100 pts.)
MATCH WORD: Jesus

MATCH GROUP
a. Fasted before being baptized by John the Baptist
b. Fasted before choosing His disciples
c. Fasted before meeting Satan

2. (200 pts.)
MATCH WORD: Moses

MATCH GROUP
a. Fasted before receiving the
Ten Commandments on Mount Sinai
b. Fasted before first confronting Pharaoh
c. Fasted before leaving Egypt for the wilderness

3. (300 pts.)
MATCH WORD: David

MATCH GROUP
a. Fasted when he heard of Amnon's death
b. Fasted when pleading for the life of his child
c. Fasted when Uriah was killed in battle

4. (400 pts.)
MATCH WORD: Paul and Barnabas

MATCH GROUP
a. Fasted after leaving prison in Philippi
b. Fasted when appointing elders in early churches
c. Fasted after the riot in Ephesus

5. (500 pts.)
MATCH WORD: John the Baptist

MATCH GROUP
a. His disciples saw no need to fast since the Pharisees fasted
b. His disciples practiced fasting
c. Once Jesus came, his disciples stopped fasting

MATCH 'EM

6. (600 pts.)
MATCH WORD: King Ahab

MATCH GROUP
a. Fasted before defeating Ben-Hadad
b. Fasted before sending prophets of Baal to meet Elijah
c. Fasted after hearing of his fate

7. (700 pts.)
MATCH WORD: Elijah

MATCH GROUP
a. Didn't eat before meeting the prophets of Baal
b. Fasted before telling Ahab of his death
c. Didn't eat on the way to Mount Horeb

8. (800 pts.)
MATCH WORD: Jesus

MATCH GROUP
a. Said to fast as the Pharisees did
b. Said to put oil on your head and wash your face
c. Said not to fast

9. (900 pts.)
MATCH WORD: Parable of two men who prayed

MATCH GROUP

a. The tax collector fasted once a week
b. The Pharisee fasted twice a week
c. The tax collector fasted twice a week

10. (1,000 pts.)
MATCH WORD: Daniel

MATCH GROUP

a. Upon arriving in Babylon, fasted instead
of eating royal food and wine
b. Fasted before interpreting Nebuchadnezzar's
first dream
c. Fasted before seeing the angel Gabriel

Quiz 28 Total Points: _____

Cumulative Score: _____

Quiz 29:

Paging Dr. Luke

1. (100 pts.)
MATCH WORD: Bleeding

MATCH GROUP
a. Peter's mother-in-law
b. Woman who touched Jesus' cloak
c. What turned Nebuchadnezzar into a wild man

2. (200 pts.)
MATCH WORD: Fever

MATCH GROUP
a. Simon's mother-in-law
b. Centurion's servant
c. Man lowered on a mat through the roof

3. (300 pts.)
MATCH WORD: Sores

MATCH GROUP
a. Eliphaz, on his stomach
b. Moses' sister, Miriam, on her stomach and back
c. Job, from his head to his soles

4. (400 pts.)
MATCH WORD: Leprosy

MATCH GROUP
a. Contracted by Aaron, who was confined outside camp for seven days
b. Contracted by Moses after delivering all plagues
c. Contracted by Miriam after she spoke against Moses

5. (500 pts.)
MATCH WORD: Boils

MATCH GROUP
a. Were caused by Moses tossing soot into the air
b. Were the third plague in Egypt
c. Affected only Pharaoh's family and livestock

6. (600 pts.)
MATCH WORD: Paralysis (Palsy)

MATCH GROUP
a. Naaman's affliction
b. Zechariah's affliction
c. Affliction of the centurion's servant

7. (700 pts.)
MATCH WORD: The lame man by the Pool of Bethesda

MATCH GROUP
a. Was healed on the Sabbath
b. Had been an invalid for eighteen years
c. Touched Jesus' hem and was healed

8. (800 pts.)
MATCH WORD: Ten men with leprosy healed by Jesus

MATCH GROUP
a. Nine were Samaritans
b. One returned to thank Jesus
c. Four returned to thank Jesus

9. (900 pts.)
MATCH WORD: Fever and dysentery

MATCH GROUP
a. Governor Felix
b. Drusilla, wife of Felix
c. Publius's father

10. (1,000 pts.)
MATCH WORD: Leprosy

MATCH GROUP
a. King Jehoram
b. King Uzziah
c. Elijah

Quiz 29 Total Points: _____

Cumulative Score: _____

Quiz 30:
Who's Who
Part IV

1. (100 pts.)

MATCH WORD: Goliath

MATCH GROUP

a. Moabites' secret weapon
b. Terror of the Ammonites
c. Giant from Gath

2. (200 pts.)

MATCH WORD: John the Baptist

MATCH GROUP

a. Was imprisoned by Herod, the tetrarch of Galilee
b. Was imprisoned by Pontius Pilate
c. Was exiled to Patmos

3. (300 pts.)
MATCH WORD: Zipporah

MATCH GROUP
a. Wife of Moses
b. Wife of Jethro
c. Wife of Gershom

4. (400 pts.)
MATCH WORD: Demetrius

MATCH GROUP
a. Silversmith in Ephesus
b. Helper of Paul in Macedonia
c. Spokesman for Jews in Ephesus

5. (500 pts.)
MATCH WORD: Haman

MATCH GROUP
a. Esther's cousin
b. Friend of Job
c. Second in command to King Xerxes

MATCH 'EM

6. (600 pts.)
MATCH WORD: Artaxerxes

MATCH GROUP
a. King of Babylon, who captured Zedekiah
b. King of Persia, who decreed Israelites
could return to Jerusalem
c. King of Judah, who renewed covenant with God

7. (700 pts.)
MATCH WORD: Hophni and Phineas

MATCH GROUP
a. Eli's sons, who died on the same day
b. Moses' sons, who were circumcised by their mother
c. Samuel's sons, who disobeyed God

8. (800 pts.)
MATCH WORD: Festus

MATCH GROUP
a. Presented religious leaders' charges against
Paul to governor of Judea
b. Succeeded Felix as governor of Judea
c. Was married to Drusilla, a Jewish woman

9. (900 pts.)
MATCH WORD: Publius

MATCH GROUP

a. Greek silversmith
b. Chief official on Malta
c. Greek preacher in early church

10. (1,000 pts.)
MATCH WORD: Hushai the Arkite

MATCH GROUP

a. Told Absalom to send twelve thousand
men to attack David's forces
b. Told Absalom to personally lead
an army against David
c. Plunged three javelins into Absalom

Quiz 30 Total Points: _____

Cumulative Score: _____

Quiz 31:
At Rest

1. (100 pts.)
MATCH WORD: Jesus

MATCH GROUP
a. Buried in a tomb with the patriarchs
b. Buried in Bethlehem
c. Buried in a garden tomb near the site of His
   crucifixion

2. (200 pts.)
MATCH WORD: Rachel

MATCH GROUP
a. Died after giving birth
b. Buried with Sarah and Abraham
c. Buried by son Joseph

3. (300 pts.)
MATCH WORD: Jesus

MATCH GROUP

a. Buried by Roman soldiers with guidance from the disciples
b. Buried by Joseph and Nicodemus
c. Buried by Mary and Mary Magdalene

4. (400 pts.)
MATCH WORD: Abraham

MATCH GROUP

a. Buried by Ishmael and Isaac
b. Buried in Jerusalem
c. Buried in the cave of Machpelah

5. (500 pts.)
MATCH WORD: Jacob

MATCH GROUP

a. Buried in a coffin in Egypt
b. Buried in Canaan by Joseph
c. Buried in Canaan by Joseph, who then stayed in Canaan

MATCH 'EM

6. (600 pts.)
MATCH WORD: Isaac

MATCH GROUP
a. Buried in Jerusalem
b. Buried by Esau and Jacob
c. Buried by Rebekah

7. (700 pts.)
MATCH WORD: Joseph

MATCH GROUP
a. Buried in Egypt with the Pharaohs
b. His bones were carried from Egypt to Shechem
c. His ashes were scattered on the Jordan River

8. (800 pts.)
MATCH WORD: Sarah

MATCH GROUP
a. Buried in Jerusalem
b. Buried on land purchased from the Hittites
c. Buried in Ur of the Chaldeans

9. (900 pts.)
MATCH WORD: Moses

MATCH GROUP

a. Buried in Moab
b. Buried in Canaan with the patriarchs
c. Buried in a coffin in Egypt

10. (1,000 pts.)
MATCH WORD: Abner

MATCH GROUP

a. Hidden away by Joab, who never
confessed to his killing
b. Buried in Jerusalem by David
c. Buried in Hebron

Quiz 31 Total Points: _____

Cumulative Score: _____

Quiz 32:
Also Known As
Part II

1. (100 pts.)
MATCH WORD: Levi

MATCH GROUP
a. Aaron
b. Matthew
c. Luke

2. (200 pts.)
MATCH WORD: Beelzebub

MATCH GROUP
a. Ahab
b. Belshazzar
c. Satan

3. (300 pts.)
MATCH WORD: Simon

MATCH GROUP
a. Andrew
b. Cephas
c. Philip

4. (400 pts.)
MATCH WORD: Joshua

MATCH GROUP
a. Hoshea
b. Jeroboam
c. Jesse

5. (500 pts.)
MATCH WORD: Naomi

MATCH GROUP
a. Mara
b. Orpah
c. Mary

6. (600 pts.)
MATCH WORD: Bethlehem

MATCH GROUP
a. Bethany
b. Emmaus
c. Ephrathah

7. (700 pts.)
MATCH WORD: Esther

MATCH GROUP
a. Hannah
b. Hagar
c. Hadassah

8. (800 pts.)
MATCH WORD: Ahasuerus

MATCH GROUP
a. Asa
b. Xerxes
c. Abijah

9. (900 pts.)
MATCH WORD: Gideon

MATCH GROUP
a. Jair
b. Joab
c. Jerub-Baal

10. (1,000 pts.)
MATCH WORD: Bar-Jesus

MATCH GROUP
a. Elymas
b. Eliezer
c. Alexander

Quiz 32 Total Points: _____

Cumulative Score: _____

Quiz 33:
The (Same) Name Game
Part II

1. (100 pts.)
MATCH WORD: Jonathan

MATCH GROUP
a. Ate honey during battle with Philistines
b. Killed by his father, Saul
c. Put to death by Saul's soldiers

2. (200 pts.)
MATCH WORD: James

MATCH GROUP
a. Brother of Andrew
b. Accompanied Jesus to Gethsemane
c. Brother of Simon Peter

3. (300 pts.)
MATCH WORD: Deborah

MATCH GROUP
a. Was judge of Israel after Gideon
b. Wife of Heber the Kenite
c. Told Barak the honor of victory would not be his

4. (400 pts.)
MATCH WORD: Eliezer

MATCH GROUP
a. Friend of Job
b. Servant of Abraham
c. High priest of Israel

5. (500 pts.)
MATCH WORD: James

MATCH GROUP
a. Spoke concerning Gentiles at Council at Jerusalem
b. Accompanied Paul on his first missionary journey
c. Was exiled to Patmos

MATCH 'EM

6. (600 pts.)
MATCH WORD: Jehu

MATCH GROUP
a. Was anointed king of Israel by Elijah
b. Commander of David's army
c. Father-in-law of Moses

7. (700 pts.)
MATCH WORD: Jehu

MATCH GROUP
a. Judge of Israel
b. Father of David
c. Prophet who spoke against King Baasha

8. (800 pts.)
MATCH WORD: Jonathan

MATCH GROUP
a. Son of Zadok
b. Son of Shimei
c. Son of Abiathar

9. (900 pts.)
MATCH WORD: Eliezer

MATCH GROUP
a. Sorcerer on Cyprus
b. Husband of Naomi
c. Son of Moses

10. (1,000 pts.)
MATCH WORD: Deborah

MATCH GROUP
a. Handmaiden of Sarah
b. Nurse of Rebekah
c. Also known as Tabitha

Quiz 33 Total Points: _____

Cumulative Score: _____

Quiz 34:

Son of Buzi

(Ezekiel)

1. (100 pts.)
MATCH WORD: Where Ezekiel prophesied

MATCH GROUP

a. Jerusalem
b. Babylon
c. Nineveh

2. (200 pts.)
MATCH WORD: Ezekiel

MATCH GROUP

a. Was told to marry an adulterous woman
b. Was told to speak first, then eat a scroll
c. Was told to eat a scroll

3. (300 pts.)
MATCH WORD: What God called Ezekiel

MATCH GROUP
a. David
b. A shepherd
c. A watchman

4. (400 pts.)
MATCH WORD: Siege of Jerusalem

MATCH GROUP
a. Described by Ezekiel in words God gave him
b. Ended by Ezekiel putting on ashes and sackcloth
c. Depicted by model Ezekiel built

5. (500 pts.)
MATCH WORD: Four creatures

MATCH GROUP
a. Man, ox, lion, eagle
b. Man, camel, lion, eagle
c. Man, ox, leopard, eagle

MATCH 'EM

6. (600 pts.)
MATCH WORD: Cooking pot

MATCH GROUP
a. The pot was filled with the poorest meat
b. Allegory given on date of siege of Jerusalem
c. The pot represented Babylon

7. (700 pts.)
MATCH WORD: Ezekiel

MATCH GROUP
a. Was told not to mourn his wife's death
b. Was told to put on ashes and sackcloth after his wife's death
c. Was told to moan loudly during his wife's funeral procession

8. (800 pts.)
MATCH WORD: Vision of Jerusalem's massacre

MATCH GROUP
a. Those spared were elders in the temple
b. Those spared had marks on their foreheads
c. Those spared were old men and young maidens

9. (900 pts.)
MATCH WORD: Oholah and Oholibah

MATCH GROUP

a. Oholibah is Jerusalem
b. Oholibah is Samaria
c. Oholah is the younger "sister"

10. (1,000 pts.)
MATCH WORD: Two sticks joined together

MATCH GROUP

a. Symbolized Judah and Ephraim
b. Symbolized Babylon and Israel
c. Symbolized Ezekiel and his wife

Quiz 34 Total Points: _____

Cumulative Score: _____

Quiz 35:
Reduced to Tears

1. (100 pts.)
MATCH WORD: Jesus

MATCH GROUP
a. Told Mary and Martha not to cry
b. Did not go to Lazarus's tomb because He knew He would cry
c. Wept at Lazarus's tomb

2. (200 pts.)
MATCH WORD: Jesus

MATCH GROUP
a. Wept over the future destruction of Jerusalem
b. Wept when he saw John the Baptist
c. Is never recorded as weeping in the Bible

3. (300 pts.)
MATCH WORD: David

MATCH GROUP
a. Cried when his sick child died
b. Cried while his sick child was still alive
c. Cried when Uriah was killed

4. (400 pts.)
MATCH WORD: Nehemiah

MATCH GROUP
a. Cried when the Book of Law was read
b. Cried when he saw Jerusalem's broken wall
c. Cried when he heard about Jerusalem's broken wall

5. (500 pts.)
MATCH WORD: Jeremiah (the weeping prophet)

MATCH GROUP
a. Died in prison in Jerusalem
b. Was thrown into a muddy cistern
c. Was taken captive to Babylon

6. (600 pts.)
MATCH WORD: Jeremiah

MATCH GROUP
a. Was beaten and put into stocks
b. Was thrown into the Valley of Ben Hinnom
c. Was exiled to Moab

7. (700 pts.)
MATCH WORD: Jeremiah

MATCH GROUP
a. Prophesied in Babylon during captivity
b. First prophesied to King Josiah of Judah
c. Was sent to Nineveh by God

8. (800 pts.)
MATCH WORD: Jeremiah's yoke

MATCH GROUP
a. Symbolized Jeremiah serving Zedekiah
b. Symbolized Nebuchadnezzar serving Zedekiah
c. Symbolized Judah serving Babylon

9. (900 pts.)
MATCH WORD: Elisha

MATCH GROUP

a. Cried when Elijah departed to heaven
b. Cried at the sight of Hazael
c. Told the Shunammite woman not to cry

10. (1,000 pts.)
MATCH WORD: Jeremiah

MATCH GROUP

a. Was told by God to buy a scarlet cord
b. Was told by God to draw Jerusalem on a clay tablet
c. Was told by God to buy a linen belt

Quiz 35 Total Points: _____

Cumulative Score: _____

Quiz 36:

Double Takes

1. (100 pts.)

MATCH WORD: Rachel

MATCH GROUP

a. Married Jacob after her older sister had also married him

b. Married Jacob before Leah got married

c. Refused to wait seven years to marry Jacob

2. (200 pts.)

MATCH WORD: Sarai

MATCH GROUP

a. Once served Pharaoh as a maidservant

b. Was taken into Pharaoh's palace because of her beauty

c. Brought wealth and health to Pharaoh

3. (300 pts.)
MATCH WORD: Bathsheba

MATCH GROUP
a. Met David at the palace with her husband
b. Was first seen by David as she bathed
c. Was the mother of David's son Adonijah

4. (400 pts.)
MATCH WORD: Bathsheba

MATCH GROUP
a. Was the "ewe lamb" in Nathan's parable
b. Would bear only one son, Solomon
c. Was put to death because of her sin

5. (500 pts.)
MATCH WORD: Rachel

MATCH GROUP
a. Was the mother of Jacob's only daughter, Dinah
b. Named her second son Benjamin
c. Named her second son Ben-Oni

6. (600 pts.)
MATCH WORD: Esther

MATCH GROUP
a. Preceded Vashti as queen of Persia
b. Told the king about her ancestry at their first meeting
c. Was one of many girls who vied to be queen of Persia

7. (700 pts.)
MATCH WORD: Sarah

MATCH GROUP
a. Became Abimelech's maidservant
b. Made a daring escape from Abimelech's household
c. Caused every woman in Abimelech's household to be barren

8. (800 pts.)
MATCH WORD: Abigail

MATCH GROUP
a. Met David when riding on a donkey
b. Lost her entire family to David's troops
c. Left her husband for David

9. (900 pts.)
MATCH WORD: Esther

MATCH GROUP
a. Was responsible for the celebration known as Feast of Trumpets
b. Was from the tribe of Benjamin
c. Gave five banquets for Haman

10. (1,000 pts.)
MATCH WORD: Abigail

MATCH GROUP
a. Was from Jezreel
b. Was from Carmel
c. Was from Hebron

Quiz 36 Total Points: _____

Cumulative Score: _____

Quiz 37:
O Jerusalem

1. (100 pts.)
MATCH WORD: Jerusalem

MATCH GROUP
a. Also known as City of David
b. Also known as City of Solomon
c. Also known as Babylon of the West

2. (200 pts.)
MATCH WORD: Jesus

MATCH GROUP
a. Walked beside a donkey on His way into Jerusalem
b. Rode into Jerusalem on a donkey
c. Led Mary on a donkey into Jerusalem

3. (300 pts.)
MATCH WORD: Nehemiah

MATCH GROUP
a. Was a scribe for Cyrus in Jerusalem
b. Kept the ark of the covenant in Jerusalem for David
c. Rebuilt Jerusalem's wall after captivity

4. (400 pts.)
MATCH WORD: Jesus

MATCH GROUP
a. Stood on the highest point of the temple in Jerusalem
b. Refused Satan's offer to stand on the highest
point of the temple in Jerusalem
c. Chose His disciples outside the temple in Jerusalem

5. (500 pts.)
MATCH WORD: Solomon

MATCH GROUP
a. Built a palace for the Queen of Sheba in Jerusalem
b. Built two temples in Jerusalem
c. Built a separate palace for Pharaoh's daughter in
Jerusalem

MATCH 'EM

6. (600 pts.)
MATCH WORD: Paul, in Jerusalem

MATCH GROUP
a. Was transferred directly from there to Rome
b. Was told by his nephew of a plot to kill him
c. Preached at the site of an idol to an unknown god

7. (700 pts.)
MATCH WORD: Nebuchadnezzar

MATCH GROUP
a. Defeated King Jehoichin and seized the city
b. Seized Jerusalem from King Zedekiah
c. Threatened but never conquered Jerusalem

8. (800 pts.)
MATCH WORD: Sennacherib

MATCH GROUP
a. Conquered Jerusalem for Assyria
b. Threatened to conquer Jerusalem
c. Was killed by an angel outside Jerusalem

9. (900 pts.)
MATCH WORD: Council in Jerusalem

MATCH GROUP
a. Decided Gentile believers should be circumcised
b. Decided Gentile believers must adhere to every law of Moses
c. Decided Gentile believers didn't have to be circumcised

10. (1,000 pts.)
MATCH WORD: New Jerusalem

MATCH GROUP
a. Has no temple
b. Has a sun and moon
c. Has gates that close at night

Quiz 37 Total Points: _____

Cumulative Score: _____

Quiz 38:
Notable Numbers
Part II

1. (100 pts.)
MATCH WORD: Thirty

MATCH GROUP
a. Age of Caleb when he was sent as a spy into Canaan
b. Age of Moses when he first spoke to Pharaoh
c. Age of Jesus when He began His ministry

2. (200 pts.)
MATCH WORD: Eighteen

MATCH GROUP
a. Number that perished in shipwreck off Malta
b. Number that perished when tower of Siloam fell
c. Number of spies sent into Canaan

3. (300 pts.)
MATCH WORD: Fifty-two

MATCH GROUP
a. Days Nehemiah spent rebuilding Jerusalem's wall
b. Days Jesus fasted in the wilderness
c. Messengers Jesus sent out as missionaries

4. (400 pts.)
MATCH WORD: Seven

MATCH GROUP
a. Age of Josiah when he became king
b. Years Solomon spent building the temple
c. Years Joash was hidden from Athaliah

5. (500 pts.)
MATCH WORD: Twelve

MATCH GROUP
a. Months of beauty treatments for Esther
b. Plagues God sent against Egypt
c. Age of Joash when he became king

MATCH 'EM

6. (600 pts.)
MATCH WORD: Four hundred

MATCH GROUP
a. Age of Adam at his death
b. Length in cubits of Solomon's palace
c. In shekels, what Abraham paid for Sarah's burial plot

7. (700 pts.)
MATCH WORD: Seven

MATCH GROUP
a. Banquets Esther hosted for Haman and Xerxes
b. Times Shunammite's son sneezed after Elisha restored his life
c. Coins widow deposited in temple treasury

8. (800 pts.)
MATCH WORD: Ten

MATCH GROUP
a. Number of daughters of Haman
b. Number of sons of Haman
c. Number of sons and daughters of Hannah and Elkanah

9. (900 pts.)
MATCH WORD: Forty

MATCH GROUP
a. Days God told Ezekiel to lie on his left side
b. Age of Jesus when He began His ministry on earth
c. Days God told Ezekiel to lie on his right side

10. (1,000 pts.)
MATCH WORD: Three hundred ninety

MATCH GROUP
a. Days God told Ezekiel to lie on his left side
b. Age of Noah at his death
c. Days God told Ezekiel to lie on his right side

Quiz 38 Total Points: _____

Cumulative Score: _____

Quiz 39:
Birds of a Feather

1. (100 pts.)
MATCH WORD: Dove

MATCH GROUP
a. Alit on Jesus after His baptism
b. Alit on John the Baptist after Jesus' baptism
c. Had an olive branch in its beak at Jesus' baptism

2. (200 pts.)
MATCH WORD: Pair of doves or young pigeons

MATCH GROUP
a. Brought by Mary when she visited Elizabeth
b. Brought by Mary and Joseph to the temple
c. Brought by Anna and Simeon when they saw Jesus

3. (300 pts.)
MATCH WORD: Dove

MATCH GROUP
a. Sent out by Noah before the raven
b. Sent out once by Noah and never returned to the ark
c. Sent out by Noah three times

4. (400 pts.)
MATCH WORD: Birds

MATCH GROUP
a. Created on the fourth day
b. Created on the third day
c. Created on the fifth day

5. (500 pts.)
MATCH WORD: Ravens

MATCH GROUP
a. Fed Elisha by the Jordan River
b. Fed Noah on Mount Ararat
c. Fed Elijah by the Kerith Ravine

MATCH 'EM

6. (600 pts.)
MATCH WORD: Raven

MATCH GROUP
a. Sent out by Noah after forty days
b. Appeared at the window of the ark after forty days
c. Did not return to Noah after forty days

7. (700 pts.)
MATCH WORD: Eagle

MATCH GROUP
a. Sent out by Noah from the ark
b. Acceptable to eat, per Old Testament law
c. One of the living creatures around the throne of heaven

8. (800 pts.)
MATCH WORD: Eagle feathers

MATCH GROUP
a. What Nebuchadnezzar wore in his crown
b. What Nebuchadnezzar's hair looked like, to fulfill his dream
c. What Nebuchadnezzar collected

9. (900 pts.)
MATCH WORD: Horned owl

MATCH GROUP
a. Acceptable to eat, per Moses' instructions
b. Unacceptable to eat, per Moses' instructions
c. To be used as part of a sacrifice for infectious skin diseases

10. (1,000 pts.)
MATCH WORD: Dove and young pigeon

MATCH GROUP
a. God commanded Abram to bring these, not cut in two
b. God commanded Abram to bring these, cut in two
c. Abram watched as birds of prey ate these

Quiz 39 Total Points: _____

Cumulative Score: _____

Quiz 40:
Who's Who
Part V

1. (100 pts.)
MATCH WORD: Lazarus

MATCH GROUP
a. Man from Bethany and friend of Jesus
b. Father-in-law of Jacob
c. Teacher in Cyrene

2. (200 pts.)
MATCH WORD: Michael

MATCH GROUP
a. Archangel of God
b. High priest of Salem
c. Wife of David

3. (300 pts.)
MATCH WORD: Enoch

MATCH GROUP
a. Father of Methuselah who walked with God
b. Son of Seth
c. Father of Noah who so named him as a source of comfort

4. (400 pts.)
MATCH WORD: Rhoda

MATCH GROUP
a. Daughter of Herodias who danced at Herod's birthday
b. Sister of Laban
c. Servant who recognized Peter's voice

5. (500 pts.)
MATCH WORD: Phoebe

MATCH GROUP
a. Wife of Felix
b. Servant or deaconess of the early church
c. Wife of Herod Agrippa

MATCH 'EM

6. (600 pts.)
MATCH WORD: Phinehas .

MATCH GROUP
a. Jailer of Paul in Philippi
b. Priest who stopped a plague against Israel
c. Son of Aaron who disobeyed God

7. (700 pts.)
MATCH WORD: Agabus

MATCH GROUP
a. Roman ruler who heard Paul's case
b. Prophet against Solomon to Jeroboam
c. Prophet who predicted famine in the Roman world

8. (800 pts.)
MATCH WORD: Peninnah

MATCH GROUP
a. Wife of Pharaoh's official
b. Wife of Elkanah
c. Son of Benaiah and leader of Israel

9. (900 pts.)
MATCH WORD: Elimelech

MATCH GROUP
a. Son of Ruth and Boaz
b. Husband of Orpah
c. Husband of Naomi

10. (1,000 pts.)
MATCH WORD: Arioch

MATCH GROUP
a. Chief of Nebuchadnezzar's court officials
b. Commander of Nebuchadnezzar's guard
c. Sold David the site for the temple

Quiz 40 Total Points: _____

Cumulative Score: _____

Quiz 41:
Cities of Refuge
Part I

1. (100 pts.)
MATCH WORD: Cana

MATCH GROUP
a. Land of Sodom and Gomorrah
b. Where Jesus turned water into wine
c. Where Paul sailed

2. (200 pts.)
MATCH WORD: Bethlehem

MATCH GROUP
a. Where Saul was anointed by Samuel
b. Where David was anointed by Samuel
c. Where Jacob built an altar

3. (300 pts.)
MATCH WORD: Capernaum

MATCH GROUP
a. Where the Shunammite woman's child was restored
   to life
b. Where Paul and Apollos preached
c. Where Jesus began His public ministry

4. (400 pts.)
MATCH WORD: Antioch

MATCH GROUP
a. Hill in Athens where Paul preached
b. Where the disciples were first called Christians
c. City of the Philistines where the ark was carried

5. (500 pts.)
MATCH WORD: Damascus

MATCH GROUP
a. Where Paul's sight was restored
b. Where the golden image of Nebuchadnezzar was
   erected
c. Where David fled, feigning madness

MATCH 'EM

6. (600 pts.)
MATCH WORD: Jericho

MATCH GROUP
a. Where Naaman's leprosy was cured
b. Burnt to the ground by the Israelites
c. Where Elijah ascended into heaven

7. (700 pts.)
MATCH WORD: Bethel

MATCH GROUP
a. Where Lazarus lived
b. Where a pool existed known for its healing powers
c. Where Jacob built an altar

8. (800 pts.)
MATCH WORD: Philippi

MATCH GROUP
a. Where Paul and Silas met Lydia
b. Capital of the Philistines
c. Home of Philip the evangelist

9. (900 pts.)
MATCH WORD: Joppa

MATCH GROUP
a. Where David reigned for a time as king
b. Where Abraham dwelt, under the trees of Mamre
c. Where Dorcas was raised from the dead

10. (1,000 pts.)
MATCH WORD: Cenchrea

MATCH GROUP
a. Where Ur was located
b. Where Paul shaved his head
c. Region named after Caesar Augustus

Quiz 41 Total Points: _____

Cumulative Score: _____

Quiz 42:
Staff of Life

1. (100 pts.)

MATCH WORD: The Lord's Supper

MATCH GROUP

a. Bread represented manna in the wilderness
b. Bread represented Jesus' body
c. Bread represented the bread of the Presence in the tabernacle

2. (200 pts.)

MATCH WORD: Satan

MATCH GROUP

a. Told Jesus to turn stones into bread
b. Gave Jesus bread to eat after He fasted
c. Tempted Jesus with loaves of freshly baked bread

3. (300 pts.)
MATCH WORD: Naomi

MATCH GROUP
a. Baked bread for her daughters-in-law
b. Heard there was bread in Judah
c. Was married to a baker of barley loaves

4. (400 pts.)
MATCH WORD: Elijah

MATCH GROUP
a. Baked bread for the widow at Zarephath
b. Served bread to the prophets of Baal
c. Was fed bread and meat by ravens

5. (500 pts.)
MATCH WORD: First Passover

MATCH GROUP
a. Raisin cakes
b. Barley bread
c. Bread without yeast

MATCH 'EM

6. (600 pts.)
MATCH WORD: Manna

MATCH GROUP
a. Stopped the day after the Israelites
ate the bread of Canaan
b. Tasted like quail
c. Continued until the Israelites conquered Jericho

7. (700 pts.)
MATCH WORD: Manna

MATCH GROUP
a. Twice a day, seven days a week
b. Once a day, six days a week
c. Once a day, seven days a week

8. (800 pts.)
MATCH WORD: Tabernacle bread

MATCH GROUP
a. Seven loaves
b. Ten loaves
c. Twelve loaves

9. (900 pts.)
MATCH WORD: Lot

MATCH GROUP
a. Baked bread without yeast for two angels
b. Refused to eat bread before Sodom was destroyed
c. Baked bread to take with him out of Sodom

10. (1,000 pts.)
MATCH WORD: Ahimelech

MATCH GROUP
a. Refused to give David bread meant
only for the priests
b. Gave David consecrated bread to eat
c. Gave Saul consecrated bread to eat

Quiz 42 Total Points: _____

Cumulative Score: _____._____

Quiz 43:
Treed

1. (100 pts.)
MATCH WORD: Garden of Eden

MATCH GROUP
a. Where Adam and Eve ate from the tree of life
b. Where Adam and Eve ate from the tree of knowledge of good and evil
c. Where the tree of life was not found

2. (200 pts.)
MATCH WORD: Zacchaeus

MATCH GROUP
a. Hid behind a sycamore tree when Jesus walked by
b. Climbed a sycamore tree to see Jesus
c. Hid behind a sycamore tree to avoid an angry mob

3. (300 pts.)
MATCH WORD: Deborah

MATCH GROUP
a. Held court under the Palm of Deborah
b. Slew Sisera under the Palm of Deborah
c. Refused to meet Barak under the Palm of Deborah

4. (400 pts.)
MATCH WORD: Abram

MATCH GROUP
a. Told Hagar to flee to the great trees of Mamre
b. Told Lot to live near the great trees of Mamre
c. Lived near the great trees of Mamre

5. (500 pts.)
MATCH WORD: Absalom

MATCH GROUP
a. Waited for Joab high up in an oak tree
b. Was killed when an oak tree fell on him
c. Caught his hair in the limbs of an oak tree

MATCH 'EM

6. (600 pts.)
MATCH WORD: Solomon

MATCH GROUP
a. Had his throne hall covered with cedar
b. Used no cedar or pine when constructing God's temple
c. Had his throne hall lined in pine

7. (700 pts.)
MATCH WORD: Gideon

MATCH GROUP
a. Cut down oak in Ophrah belonging to his father
b. Judged Israel from under oak in Ophrah
c. Was visited by an angel under oak in Ophrah

8. (800 pts.)
MATCH WORD: David

MATCH GROUP
a. Attacked Philistines in front of balsam trees
b. Planted a balsam tree in the Valley of Rephaim
c. Planted a balsam tree in memory of Absalom

9. (900 pts.)
MATCH WORD: Amos

MATCH GROUP
a. Prophet's son
b. Shepherd who took care of sycamore trees
c. Prophet who sat under a sycamore tree

10. (1,000 pts.)
MATCH WORD: Oak below Bethel

MATCH GROUP
a. Where Rebekah was buried
b. Where Rebekah's nurse was buried
c. Where Esau was buried

Quiz 43 Total Points: _____

Cumulative Score: _____

Quiz 44:
Not Same Old, Same Old

1. (100 pts.)
MATCH WORD: Moses

MATCH GROUP
a. Saw the angel of God lead the way across the Red Sea
b. With God's help, stretched out his hand, and the Red Sea was divided
c. With God's help, stretched out his hand, and the Jordan River was divided

2. (200 pts.)
MATCH WORD: John the Baptist

MATCH GROUP
a. Saw Jesus' face become "radiant" after His baptism
b. Saw an eagle alight on Jesus' shoulder after His baptism
c. Heard God's voice from heaven speak after Jesus' baptism

3. (300 pts.)
MATCH WORD: The apostles

MATCH GROUP
a. Saw Jesus rising in the air up to heaven
b. Saw angels accompany Jesus to heaven
c. Saw Jesus walk down the road to Emmaus and vanish

4. (400 pts.)
MATCH WORD: Aaron and the Israelites

MATCH GROUP
a. Witnessed Moses' "radiant" face when he descended
from Mount Sinai
b. Witnessed the "radiance" of the two tablets Moses
brought from God
c. Saw Moses descend with two angels
from Mount Sinai

5. (500 pts.)
MATCH WORD: Peter, James, and John

MATCH GROUP
a. Witnessed the appearance of Elisha and Moses with
Jesus
b. Witnessed the appearance of Elijah and Abraham
with Jesus
c. Saw Jesus' face shine like the sun and His clothes
become white

MATCH 'EM

6. (600 pts.)
MATCH WORD: Jesus' crucifixion

MATCH GROUP
a. The sun stopped in the middle of the sky
b. The temple curtain was torn in two from top to bottom
c. The Nile River was turned to blood

7. (700 pts.)
MATCH WORD: King Belshazzar

MATCH GROUP
a. Saw three men survive a fiery furnace
b. Saw human fingers, without a body, write words on a wall
c. Saw talons sprout from his fingertips

8. (800 pts.)
MATCH WORD: Hezekiah

MATCH GROUP
a. Saw the shadow on a sundial go forward ten steps
b. Saw the shadow on a sundial go backward ten steps
c. Experienced total darkness at noon

9. (900 pts.)
MATCH WORD: Joshua

MATCH GROUP
a. Saw the sun stop in the middle of the sky
b. Saw night last for a full day
c. Saw the sun stop in the middle of the sky for two full days

10. (1,000 pts.)
MATCH WORD: Gideon

MATCH GROUP
a. Squeezed a fleece and got two bowlfuls of water
b. Saw an angel set fire to an Asherah pole
c. Saw a rock set on fire by an angel

Quiz 44 Total Points: _____

Cumulative Score: _____

Quiz 45:
Come Again?

1. (100 pts.)
MATCH WORD: Centurion

MATCH GROUP
a. Commander of 1,000 soldiers
b. Commander of 100 soldiers
c. Commander of 150 soldiers

2. (200 pts.)
MATCH WORD: Hyssop

MATCH GROUP
a. Babylonian fortress
b. Egyptian song
c. Plant with stalks

3. (300 pts.)
MATCH WORD: Kinsman-redeemer

MATCH GROUP
a. Close relative who took responsibility for family
b. Brother of widow's husband
c. Nephew of widow's husband

4. (400 pts.)
MATCH WORD: Ephod

MATCH GROUP
a. Dry measure
b. God of the Hittites
c. Linen garment worn by priests

5. (500 pts.)
MATCH WORD: Freedmen

MATCH GROUP
a. Roman slaves who became Christians
b. Jewish slaves who formed their own synagogue
c. Jewish slaves who became Christians

6. (600 pts.)
MATCH WORD: Higgaion

MATCH GROUP
a. Musical direction or meditation
b. God of the Hermonites
c. Loud exclamation or enthusiastic praise

7. (700 pts.)
MATCH WORD: Shibboleth

MATCH GROUP
a. A grove of acacia trees
b. A stream
c. City of the Shimronites

8. (800 pts.)
MATCH WORD: Nephilim

MATCH GROUP
a. Cain's descendants
b. Naphtali's descendants
c. Giants

9. (900 pts.)
MATCH WORD: Corban

MATCH GROUP
a. Offering made to avoid helping needy parents
b. Vow made to offer money to widows
c. Tithe made to temple at Ephesus

10. (1,000 pts.)
MATCH WORD: Stairway of Ahaz

MATCH GROUP
a. A stone formation
b. A sundial
c. A constellation

Quiz 45 Total Points: _____

Cumulative Score: _____

Quiz 46:
At Sea (or River)

1. (100 pts.)
MATCH WORD: Nile

MATCH GROUP
a. Where baby Moses was hidden
b. Was turned to mud by Moses
c. Also known as the Great Sea

2. (200 pts.)
MATCH WORD: Galilee

MATCH GROUP
a. Where Jesus was baptized
b. Where Jesus first met Matthew
c. Where Jesus walked on water

3. (300 pts.)
MATCH WORD: River of Life

MATCH GROUP
a. In the New Jerusalem
b. Another name for the Tigris
c. Another name for the Jordan

4. (400 pts.)
MATCH WORD: Euphrates

MATCH GROUP
a. One of three headwaters of Eden
b. One of four headwaters of Eden
c. The only river in Eden

5. (500 pts.)
MATCH WORD: Tigris

MATCH GROUP
a. What Aaron struck and turned to blood
b. One of four headwaters of Eden
c. One of three headwaters of Eden

MATCH 'EM

6. (600 pts.)
MATCH WORD: Kerith

MATCH GROUP
a. Where Elisha threw Elijah's cloak
b. Where Elisha met Elijah
c. Where Elijah drank from the brook

7. (700 pts.)
MATCH WORD: Jordan

MATCH GROUP
a. Near the plain where Lot chose to live
b. Where Jesus walked on water
c. Near the plain where Abram chose to live

8. (800 pts.)
MATCH WORD: Kebar

MATCH GROUP
a. Where Jeremiah received God's prophecy
b. Where Ezekiel received God's prophecy
c. A river in northern Israel

9. (900 pts.)
MATCH WORD: Jabbok

MATCH GROUP
a. What Joshua crossed to enter Canaan
b. Near where Jacob wrestled with God
c. Called the border of the Canaanites

10. (1,000 pts.)
MATCH WORD: Merom

MATCH GROUP
a. Where Moses struck the rock for water
b. Where Haggai received God's prophecy
c. Where the northern kings camped to attack Israel

Quiz 46 Total Points: _____

Cumulative Score: _____

Quiz 47:
With a Song in My Heart

1. (100 pts.)
MATCH WORD: Shepherds

MATCH GROUP
a. Sang for joy upon seeing angels outside Bethlehem
b. Sang to their sheep after seeing baby Jesus
c. Were sung to by angels outside Bethlehem

2. (200 pts.)
MATCH WORD: Mary

MATCH GROUP
a. Sang to Elizabeth after her baby leaped in her womb
b. Sang to Joseph after her baby leaped in her womb
c. Sang to the angel Gabriel

3. (300 pts.)
MATCH WORD: Moses

MATCH GROUP
a. Sang to Pharaoh to be set free
b. Sang to the Lord after the Red Sea crossing
c. Sang to the Israelites in anger after they built the
   golden calf

4. (400 pts.)
MATCH WORD: Israelites

MATCH GROUP
a. Sang about receiving water in the desert
b. Sang about receiving manna in the desert
c. Sang about the bronze snake erected by Moses

5. (500 pts.)
MATCH WORD: Moses

MATCH GROUP
a. His final song was taught to the people by Joshua
b. His final song was given him by God
c. Miriam sang his final song as a solo to the people

MATCH 'EM

6. (600 pts.)
MATCH WORD: Deborah

MATCH GROUP
a. Sang a song of victory with Barak
b. Sang a song of victory with Jael
c. Her song celebrated victory over Eglon, king of Moab

7. (700 pts.)
MATCH WORD: Hannah

MATCH GROUP
a. Sang upon learning she was pregnant
b. Sang after leaving Samuel with Eli
c. Sang to Eli upon learning of God's blessing

8. (800 pts.)
MATCH WORD: Simeon

MATCH GROUP
a. Sang a song of joy with Anna upon leaving the temple
b. Sang praises to God while holding the baby Jesus
c. Sang praises upon entering the temple the day he saw the baby Jesus

9. (900 pts.)
MATCH WORD: Song of the Lamb

MATCH GROUP

a. Sung before the seventh trumpet sounded
b. Sung by the two witnesses in Jerusalem
c. Sung before the final seven bowl judgments

10. (1,000 pts.)
MATCH WORD: Song of believers

MATCH GROUP

a. Sung by angels to the church in Sardis
b. Sung after the Lamb opened the first of seven seals
c. Sung by four creatures and
twenty-four elders to the Lamb

Quiz 47 Total Points: _____

Cumulative Score: _____

Quiz 48:
The Perils of Paul

1. (100 pts.)
MATCH WORD: First missionary journey

MATCH GROUP
a. Left initially from Jerusalem
b. Traveled with Barnabas and John Mark
c. Went first to Iconium

2. (200 pts.)
MATCH WORD: First missionary journey

MATCH GROUP
a. Barnabas left Paul at Perga
b. Paul healed a lame man in Antioch
c. Encountered Jewish sorcerer Bar-Jesus

3. (300 pts.)
MATCH WORD: Second missionary journey

MATCH GROUP
a. Traveled with Barnabas and John Mark
b. Traveled with Silas and Timothy
c. Sailed first to Cyprus

4. (400 pts.)
MATCH WORD: Second missionary journey

MATCH GROUP
a. Was thrown into prison at Philippi
b. Decided against going to Macedonia,
despite his vision
c. Was thrown into prison at Troas

5. (500 pts.)
MATCH WORD: Second missionary journey

MATCH GROUP
a. Was stoned in Athens
b. Preached first in every city to the Gentiles
c. Met Priscilla and Aquila in Corinth

MATCH 'EM

6. (600 pts.)

MATCH WORD: Third missionary journey

MATCH GROUP
a. Went first to Lystra
b. Traveled to Ephesus with Apollos
c. His handkerchiefs healed in Ephesus

7. (700 pts.)

MATCH WORD: Third missionary journey

MATCH GROUP
a. Was stoned in Ephesus
b. Brought Eutychus back to life
c. Met Agabus the prophet in Jerusalem

8. (800 pts.)

MATCH WORD: Journey to Rome

MATCH GROUP
a. Was spared flogging in Jerusalem
b. Walked into an ambush by Jews in Jerusalem
c. Was kept under guard at Felix's house

9. (900 pts.)
MATCH WORD: Journey to Rome

MATCH GROUP
a. Was set free by King Agrippa
b. Encountered a hurricane off the coast of Crete
c. Landed on Cyprus to avoid the storm

10. (1,000 pts.)
MATCH WORD: Journey to Rome

MATCH GROUP
a. Of 276 on board, 18 were lost at sea
b. Stayed on Malta for six months
c. Shook a snake into the fire on Malta

Quiz 48 Total Points: _____

Cumulative Score: _____

Quiz 49:
Ties That Bind

1. (100 pts.)
MATCH WORD: Aaron, to Moses

MATCH GROUP
a. Nephew
b. Brother
c. Cousin

2. (200 pts.)
MATCH WORD: Ishmael, to Isaac

MATCH GROUP
a. Cousin
b. Stepbrother
c. Half brother

3. (300 pts.)
MATCH WORD: Seth, to Adam

MATCH GROUP
a. Stepson
b. Nephew
c. Son

4. (400 pts.)
MATCH WORD: Asher, to Jacob

MATCH GROUP
a. Son
b. Son-in-law
c. Nephew

5. (500 pts.)
MATCH WORD: Mephibosheth, to Saul

MATCH GROUP
a. Great-nephew
b. Great-grandson
c. Grandson

MATCH 'EM

6. (600 pts.)
MATCH WORD: Dinah, to Rebekah

MATCH GROUP
a. Stepdaughter
b. Granddaughter
c. Great-granddaughter

7. (700 pts.)
MATCH WORD: Benjamin, to Ephraim

MATCH GROUP
a. Uncle
b. Grandfather
c. Cousin

8. (800 pts.)
MATCH WORD: Ruth, to Tamar

MATCH GROUP
a. Great-grandmother
b. Great-great-grandmother
c. Great-aunt

9. (900 pts.)
MATCH WORD: Nathan, to David

MATCH GROUP

a. Son
b. Stepson
c. Half brother

10. (1,000 pts.)
MATCH WORD: Joab, to David

MATCH GROUP

a. Great-nephew
b. Stepson
c. Nephew

Quiz 49 Total Points: _____

Cumulative Score: _____

Quiz 50:
Who's Who
Part VI

1. (100 pts.)
MATCH WORD: Rahab

MATCH GROUP
a. Prostitute
b. Prophetess
c. Purveyor of fine linen

2. (200 pts.)
MATCH WORD: Caiaphas

MATCH GROUP
a. Another name for Peter
b. High priest who tore his clothes
after questioning Jesus
c. One of the travelers to Emmaus with Jesus

3. (300 pts.)
MATCH WORD: Cyrus

MATCH GROUP
a. King of Babylon who literally saw the writing on the wall
b. King who wrote the proclamation to rebuild the temple in Jerusalem
c. Governor of Judaea

4. (400 pts.)
MATCH WORD: Korah

MATCH GROUP
a. Levite who rebelled against Moses
b. Benjamite who wanted to lead the Israelites
c. Half brother of Ishmael

5. (500 pts.)
MATCH WORD: Stephen

MATCH GROUP
a. Disciple exiled to Patmos
b. Member of the Synagogue of the Freedmen
c. One of seven disciples chosen to distribute food

6. (600 pts.)
MATCH WORD: Silas

MATCH GROUP
a. Went to Athens initially with Paul
b. Helped write the book of James
c. Was in jail with Paul in Philippi

7. (700 pts.)
MATCH WORD: Onesimus

MATCH GROUP
a. Accompanied Paul on his second missionary journey
b. Slave of Philemon
c. Believer who helped Paul in Ephesus

8. (800 pts.)
MATCH WORD: Abishag

MATCH GROUP
a. Daughter of Bathsheba and David
b. One of Solomon's harem
c. Requested in marriage by Adonijah

9. (900 pts.)
MATCH WORD: Ashpenaz

MATCH GROUP
a. Israelite held captive with Daniel in Babylon
b. Chief of Nebuchadnezzar's court officials
c. Commander of Nebuchadnezzar's guard

10. (1,000 pts.)
MATCH WORD: Julius

MATCH GROUP
a. Apostle who was in prison with Paul
b. Inventor of the harp and flute
c. Roman centurion who saved Paul's life

Quiz 50 Total Points: _____

Cumulative Score: _____

Quiz 51:
The (Same) Name Game
Part III

1. (100 pts.)

MATCH WORD: Judas

MATCH GROUP

a. Jesus gave him a piece of bread dipped in a dish
b. Was called a lion's cub by Jacob
c. Candidate, with Matthias, to become a disciple

2. (200 pts.)

MATCH WORD: Philip

MATCH GROUP

a. Clarified a passage from Isaiah for a eunuch
b. Owner of Onesimus
c. Witness to Jesus' transfiguration

3. (300 pts.)
MATCH WORD: Abimelech

MATCH GROUP
a. Isaac's son Esau married his daughter
b. Isaac told him Rebekah was his sister
c. Commander of Saul's army

4. (400 pts.)
MATCH WORD: Alexander

MATCH GROUP
a. Metalworker who harmed Timothy
b. Disciple who was sent to minister to Paul at Damascus
c. Teacher in the early church in Antioch

5. (500 pts.)
MATCH WORD: Judas

MATCH GROUP
a. Barnabas was called this in Lystra
b. Brother of James and author of Jude
c. Fellow prisoner of Paul in Rome

MATCH 'EM

6. (600 pts.)
MATCH WORD: Eleazar

MATCH GROUP
a. Steward of the house of Abraham
b. Son of Aaron and priest of Israel
c. Chief minister of Hezekiah

7. (700 pts.)
MATCH WORD: Eleazar

MATCH GROUP
a. Husband of Naomi
b. One of Job's friends
c. Son of Abinadab, who housed the ark of the covenant

8. (800 pts.)
MATCH WORD: Abimelech

MATCH GROUP
a. Son of the judge Gideon
b. Received the ark of God from the Philistines
c. With Korah, rebelled against Moses

9. (900 pts.)
MATCH WORD: Philip

MATCH GROUP

a. False teacher, according to Timothy
b. Son of Eli
c. Brother of Herod the tetrarch

10. (1,000 pts.)
MATCH WORD: Alexander

MATCH GROUP

a. One of Jesus' original twelve apostles
b. Member of the Jewish council who
condemned Peter and John
c. King of Judah who was defeated by Joash

Quiz 51 Total Points: _____

Cumulative Score: _____

Quiz 52:
Cities of Refuge
Part II

1. (100 pts.)
MATCH WORD: Nazareth

MATCH GROUP
a. Located in Samaria
b. Located on the Sea of Galilee
c. Where Jesus spent His boyhood

2. (200 pts.)
MATCH WORD: Athens

MATCH GROUP
a. Where Paul spent his boyhood
b. Where Jason's house was located
c. Where Paul spoke of an idol to an unknown god

3. (300 pts.)
MATCH WORD: Bethany

MATCH GROUP

a. Where Jesus ascended to heaven
b. Where Jesus fed the 5,000
c. Where Jesus told His disciples to find a donkey tied there

4. (400 pts.)
MATCH WORD: Hebron

MATCH GROUP

a. Where Lot chose to live
b. Where Abimelech and Abraham swore an oath
c. Near the Cave of Machpelah

5. (500 pts.)
MATCH WORD: Gaza

MATCH GROUP

a. Where Samson asked to die with the Philistines
b. Where Samson met his wife
c. A city of Benjamin

MATCH 'EM

6. (600 pts.)
MATCH WORD: Ramah

MATCH GROUP
a. Where Elisha trapped blinded Arameans
b. Where Samuel was born
c. Where Elijah went up to heaven in a whirlwind

7. (700 pts.)
MATCH WORD: Beersheba

MATCH GROUP
a. Where Naaman was healed of leprosy
b. Where Samuel was raised in the temple
c. Where Elijah fled to escape Jezebel

8. (800 pts.)
MATCH WORD: Tyre

MATCH GROUP
a. Where Peter restored Tabitha to life
b. Where Jesus restored a widow's son to life
c. Where Jesus healed a demon-possessed girl

9. (900 pts.)
MATCH WORD: Rome

MATCH GROUP
a. Where Paul was unable to meet with Jewish leaders
b. Where Claudius ordered Jews to leave
c. Where Jesus was crucified

10. (1,000 pts.)
MATCH WORD: Hebron

MATCH GROUP
a. Where Aaron died
b. Given to Caleb by Joshua
c. Where David reigned as king of Israel

Quiz 52 Total Points: _____

Cumulative Score: _____

Quiz 53:
Birth of a Nation
(Abraham's Journey)

1. (100 pts.)
MATCH WORD: Ur of the Chaldeans

MATCH GROUP
a. Where Terah died
b. Where Abram's brother Haran died
c. Where Sarai's name was changed to Sarah

2. (200 pts.)
MATCH WORD: Haran

MATCH GROUP
a. Where Lot chose to live
b. Where Abraham and Sarah had Isaac
c. Where Terah decided to settle

3. (300 pts.)
MATCH WORD: Shechem

MATCH GROUP
a. Where the great tree of Moreh is located
b. Where Terah died
c. A city in the Negev

4. (400 pts.)
MATCH WORD: Bethel

MATCH GROUP
a. Where Abram first built an altar in Canaan
b. Where Abram built an altar
c. Where Lot chose to live apart from Abram

5. (500 pts.)
MATCH WORD: Detour to Egypt

MATCH GROUP
a. Because of a famine
b. Because of a drought
c. Because Lot wanted to meet Pharaoh

MATCH 'EM

6. (600 pts.)
MATCH WORD: Detour to Egypt

MATCH GROUP
a. Where Abram was mistreated by Pharaoh
b. Where Abram met the king of Sodom
c. Where Pharaoh's household suffered many diseases

7. (700 pts.)
MATCH WORD: Lot

MATCH GROUP
a. Chose to live near Zoar
b. Chose to live in the land of Canaan
c. Separated from Abram in Egypt

8. (800 pts.)
MATCH WORD: Abram

MATCH GROUP
a. Chose to live between Bethel and Ai
b. Moved his tents to Hebron
c. Moved his tents back to Shechem

9. (900 pts.)
MATCH WORD: Abram

MATCH GROUP
a. Defeated King Kedorlaomer
b. Defeated the kings of Sodom and Gomorrah
c. Rescued Lot from the tar pits of the Valley of Siddim

10. (1,000 pts.)
MATCH WORD: Melchizedek

MATCH GROUP
a. King of Sodom
b. Was given a tenth of what Abram recovered
c. King of Gomorrah

Quiz 53 Total Points: _____

Cumulative Score: _____

Quiz 54:

A Promise
Is a Promise

1. (100 pts.)

MATCH WORD: Rainbow

MATCH GROUP

a. Sign of promise to Abraham
b. Sign of promise to Adam
c. Sign of promise to Noah

2. (200 pts.)

MATCH WORD: Abram

MATCH GROUP

a. Was promised land
b. Was promised twelve sons
c. Was promised three wives

3. (300 pts.)
MATCH WORD: Abram

MATCH GROUP
a. Was promised a daughter
b. Was promised a son
c. Was promised that he would live to see his grandsons

4. (400 pts.)
MATCH WORD: Jacob

MATCH GROUP
a. Was promised peace with his brother, Esau
b. Was promised numerous descendants
c. Was promised he would have peace with Egypt

5. (500 pts.)
MATCH WORD: Solomon

MATCH GROUP
a. Was promised the hand of Pharaoh's daughter
b. Was promised wisdom and great wealth
c. Was promised the favor of the Queen of Sheba

MATCH 'EM

6. (600 pts.)
MATCH WORD: Jesus

MATCH GROUP
a. Promised rest for our souls
b. Promised great material wealth to all believers
c. Promised salvation based on good works alone

7. (700 pts.)
MATCH WORD: Jesus

MATCH GROUP
a. Made no promises about the Holy Spirit
b. Promised eternal life if we believe in Him
c. Promised His coming would bring peace to families

8. (800 pts.)
MATCH WORD: Jesus' resurrection
and defeat of Satan

MATCH GROUP
a. Promised first in Genesis
b. Promised first in Exodus
c. Promised first in Psalms

9. (900 pts.)
MATCH WORD: Jesus

MATCH GROUP

a. Promised that the greatest on earth would be greatest in heaven
b. Promised the Pharisees long life
c. Promised disciples would one day sit on twelve thrones

10. (1,000 pts.)
MATCH WORD: David

MATCH GROUP

a. Was promised that his kingdom would endure forever
b. Was promised by God that he would build the temple
c. Was promised by God that Adonijah would build the temple

Quiz 54 Total Points: _____

Cumulative Score: _____

Quiz 55:
Also Known As
Part III

1. (100 pts.)
MATCH WORD: Immanuel

MATCH GROUP
a. Jesus
b. Isaiah
c. Jeremiah

2. (200 pts.)
MATCH WORD: Lucifer

MATCH GROUP
a. Lucius
b. Lucas
c. Satan

3. (300 pts.)
MATCH WORD: Salt Sea

MATCH GROUP
a. Dead Sea
b. Aegean Sea
c. Mediterranean Sea

4. (400 pts.)
MATCH WORD: Great Sea

MATCH GROUP
a. Mediterranean Sea
b. Adriatic Sea
c. Aegean Sea

5. (500 pts.)
MATCH WORD: Dorcas

MATCH GROUP
a. Drusilla
b. Tamar
c. Tabitha

MATCH 'EM

6. (600 pts.)
MATCH WORD: Mark

MATCH GROUP
a. Menahem
b. Joah
c. John

7. (700 pts.)
MATCH WORD: Cush

MATCH GROUP
a. Egypt
b. Ethiopia
c. Assyria

8. (800 pts.)
MATCH WORD: Uzziah

MATCH GROUP
a. Uzai
b. Azaniah
c. Azariah

9. (900 pts.)
MATCH WORD: Solomon

MATCH GROUP
a. Sidon
b. Jedidiah
c. Jedidah

10. (1,000 pts.)
MATCH WORD: Mattaniah

MATCH GROUP
a. Matthew
b. Zedekiah
c. Matthias

Quiz 55 Total Points: _____

Cumulative Score: _____

Quiz 56:
Just about Jesus

1. (100 pts.)
MATCH WORD: Tempted by Satan

MATCH GROUP
a. To command lizards to become bread
b. To worship Satan
c. To drown in the Sea of Galilee

2. (200 pts.)
MATCH WORD: Demons' request of Him

MATCH GROUP
a. To be sent into a herd of pigs
b. To be thrown off a cliff
c. To be drowned in the sea

3. (300 pts.)
MATCH WORD: His sign for the Pharisees

MATCH GROUP
a. Sign of catastrophic weather
b. Sign of beheading of John the Baptist
c. Sign of Jonah

4. (400 pts.)
MATCH WORD: Where He met
the woman at the well

MATCH GROUP
a. Sychar, in Samaria
b. Capernaum, in Judea
c. Tyre, in Samaria

5. (500 pts.)
MATCH WORD: Powers He gave the disciples

MATCH GROUP
a. To drive out demons and restore sight
b. To drive out demons and heal all diseases
c. To heal all diseases

6. (600 pts.)

MATCH WORD: His clearing of the temple

MATCH GROUP
a. Once
b. Twice
c. Three times

7. (700 pts.)

MATCH WORD: Attempted stoning by Jews

MATCH GROUP
a. Because Jesus healed on the Sabbath
b. Because Jesus claimed to be God
c. Because Jesus cleared the temple

8. (800 pts.)

MATCH WORD: Sermon on the Mount

MATCH GROUP
a. The meek will inherit the earth
b. The poor in spirit will be comforted
c. The peacemakers will see God

9. (900 pts.)
MATCH WORD: Earthly ancestors

MATCH GROUP
a. Deborah
b. Hannah
c. Rahab

10. (1,000 pts.)
MATCH WORD: Denounced what cities

MATCH GROUP
a. Korazin and Bethsaida
b. Korazin and Capernaum
c. Korazin, Bethsaida, and Capernaum

Quiz 56 Total Points: _____

Cumulative Score: _____

Quiz 57:
Passion Week

1. (100 pts.)
MATCH WORD: Triumphal entry

MATCH GROUP
a. Into Bethany
b. Into Jerusalem
c. Into Bethphage

2. (200 pts.)
MATCH WORD: Anointing of Jesus

MATCH GROUP
a. Done by Martha, Lazarus's sister
b. Done by pouring perfume on His head
c. Done at the home of Lazarus in Bethany

3. (300 pts.)
MATCH WORD: Judas Iscariot's betrayal

MATCH GROUP
a. For forty pieces of silver
b. Financed by the chief priests
c. Arranged a week before the Last Supper

4. (400 pts.)
MATCH WORD: Jesus' crucifixion

MATCH GROUP
a. Jesus' legs were broken by soldiers
b. Only water flowed from His pierced side
c. Occurred the day before the Sabbath

5. (500 pts.)
MATCH WORD: Garden of Gethsemane

MATCH GROUP
a. All twelve disciples accompanied Jesus
b. All of the disciples came except Judas Iscariot
c. Jesus found the disciples sleeping three times

MATCH 'EM

6. (600 pts.)

MATCH WORD: Jesus' resurrection

MATCH GROUP

a. Soldiers refused the money of the chief priests to say they moved His body
b. An angel told the women to meet Jesus in Galilee
c. Jesus appeared first to His disciples

7. (700 pts.)

MATCH WORD: The Lord's Supper (Passover)

MATCH GROUP

a. Arranged by two disciples following a man with a jar of water
b. Not attended by Judas Iscariot
c. Not attended by Simon Peter

8. (800 pts.)

MATCH WORD: Clearing of the temple

MATCH GROUP

a. On the same day as the triumphal entry
b. On the same day as the Olivet Discourse
c. On the day after the triumphal entry

9. (900 pts.)

MATCH WORD: Judas Iscariot's betrayal

MATCH GROUP

a. Soldiers came to arrest Jesus unarmed
b. Soldiers attacked Jesus with clubs
c. Judas identified Jesus with the word "Rabbi" and a
   kiss

10. (1,000 pts.)

MATCH WORD: Jesus' trial

MATCH GROUP

a. He appeared first before Annas
b. He appeared first before Caiaphas
c. He appeared first before the Sanhedrin

Quiz 57 Total Points: _____

Cumulative Score: _____

Quiz 58:

Welcome Wagon

1. (100 pts.)
MATCH WORD: Abraham

MATCH GROUP
a. Hosted three angels before the fall of Sodom
b. Hosted angels after the fall of Sodom
c. Hosted Lot before the Sodom's fall

2. (200 pts.)
MATCH WORD: Lot

MATCH GROUP
a. Hosted Nahor and Abraham before Sodom's fall
b. Hosted two angels before Sodom's fall
c. Gave two angels his home while he slept elsewhere

3. (300 pts.)
MATCH WORD: Laban

MATCH GROUP
a. Hosted Abraham's servant
b. Hosted Abraham on his search for Isaac's bride
c. Hosted Sarah and Abraham

4. (400 pts.)
MATCH WORD: Reuel

MATCH GROUP
a. Hosted Jacob fleeing Esau
b. Hosted Jacob's brothers on their way to Egypt
c. Hosted Moses, who had fled Pharaoh

5. (500 pts.)
MATCH WORD: Job

MATCH GROUP
a. Hosted everyone who had known him after his testing
b. Prepared a special feast for Eliphaz the Temanite
c. Before his testing, hosted lavish feasts for his seven
   sons and three daughters

MATCH 'EM

6. (600 pts.)
MATCH WORD: Samuel

MATCH GROUP
a. Hosted Saul and his father at Gibeah
b. Hosted Saul at his home in Jabesh
c. Hosted Saul and his servant before his anointing

7. (700 pts.)
MATCH WORD: Nehemiah

MATCH GROUP
a. Hosted Artaxerxes in Jerusalem
b. Prepared a fattened calf and sheep for Sanballat and Tobiah
c. Every day in Judah hosted 150 at his table

8. (800 pts.)
MATCH WORD: David

MATCH GROUP
a. Gave bread and cakes to the Israelites after the ark came to Jerusalem
b. Prepared a fattened calf for Uzzah
c. Gave bread and cakes to Michal after the ark came to Jerusalem

9. (900 pts.)
MATCH WORD: Manoah

MATCH GROUP
a. Fed an angel, who predicted Samson's birth
b. Prepared a burnt offering during an angel's visit
c. Hosted Gideon and his father

10. (1,000 pts.)
MATCH WORD: Gaius

MATCH GROUP
a. To John, was second in hospitality only to Diotrephes
b. Showed hospitality to traveling Christians
c. Was reprimanded for not being more hospitable

Quiz 58 Total Points: _____

Cumulative Score: _____

Quiz 59:
Ties That Bind

1. (100 pts.)
MATCH WORD: Zechariah, to John the Baptist

MATCH GROUP
a. Father
b. Uncle
c. Cousin

2. (200 pts.)
MATCH WORD: Mordecai, to Esther

MATCH GROUP
a. Brother
b. Uncle
c. Cousin

3. (300 pts.)
MATCH WORD: Samson, to Manoah

MATCH GROUP
a. Father
b. Brother
c. Son

4. (400 pts.)
MATCH WORD: Rebekah, to Abraham

MATCH GROUP
a. Granddaughter
b. Great-niece
c. Second cousin

5. (500 pts.)
MATCH WORD: Zeresh, to Haman

MATCH GROUP
a. Wife
b. Daughter
c. Sister

MATCH 'EM

6. (600 pts.)

MATCH WORD: Uzzah, to Abinadab

MATCH GROUP
a. Brother
b. Son
c. Father

7. (700 pts.)

MATCH WORD: Lamech, to Jubal and Jabal

MATCH GROUP
a. Father
b. Brother
c. Grandfather

8. (800 pts.)

MATCH WORD: Ithamar, to Aaron

MATCH GROUP
a. Nephew
b. Son
c. Grandson

9. (900 pts.)
MATCH WORD: Ichabod, to Eli

MATCH GROUP
a. Son
b. Brother
c. Grandson

10. (1,000 pts.)
MATCH WORD: Daughters of Zelophehad,
to Manasseh

MATCH GROUP
a. Great-great-granddaughters
b. Granddaughters
c. Great-great-great-granddaughters

Quiz 59 Total Points: _____

Cumulative Score: _____

Quiz 60:
A Final Who's Who

1. (100 pts.)

MATCH WORD: Pontius Pilate

MATCH GROUP

a. Had Barabbas crucified with Jesus
b. High priest and member of the Sanhedrin
c. Had notice prepared and fastened to Jesus' cross

2. (200 pts.)

MATCH WORD: Hannah

MATCH GROUP

a. Died after giving birth to Ichabod
b. Prophetess of Israel
c. Promised God her son would serve Him

3. (300 pts.)
MATCH WORD: Barnabas

MATCH GROUP
a. Brought Saul from Tarsus to Antioch
b. Was put in prison with Peter in Jerusalem
c. Prophet who predicted a severe famine throughout
the Roman world

4. (400 pts.)
MATCH WORD: Joab

MATCH GROUP
a. Killed Absalom against David's orders
b. Plotted with Absalom against David
c. Refused to send Uriah to the front lines of battle

5. (500 pts.)
MATCH WORD: Timothy

MATCH GROUP
a. Accompanied Paul on his first missionary journey
b. Was circumcised by Paul because his father was Greek
c. Had a sharp disagreement with Paul and ministered
with Barnabas

MATCH 'EM

6. (600 pts.)
MATCH WORD: Abner

MATCH GROUP
a. Commander of Saul's army
b. Was slain by Ish-bosheth
c. Refused to make an agreement with David

7. (700 pts.)
MATCH WORD: Ben-Hadad

MATCH GROUP
a. Was killed in battle by Ahab
b. His death at the hands of Hazael was predicted by Elisha
c. His death at the hands of Hazael was predicted by Elijah

8. (800 pts.)
MATCH WORD: Abishai

MATCH GROUP
a. Son of Joab
b. Accompanied David to the sleeping Saul's tent
c. One of David's three mighty men

9. (900 pts.)
MATCH WORD: Lot

MATCH GROUP
a. Was turned into a pillar of salt with his wife
b. Gave his daughters to two angels for their protection
c. His sons became the fathers of the Moabites and Ammonites

10. (1,000 pts.)
MATCH WORD: Titus

MATCH GROUP
a. Was supposed to meet Paul in Troas
b. Was left by Paul on the island of Malta
c. Was raised from the dead at Troas

Quiz 60 Total Points: _____

Cumulative Score: _____

A perfect score for *Bible Trivia Challenge: Match 'Em* is 330,000 points. . . . How well did you match wits?

Answer Key

QUIZ 1: WHO'S WHO
1. C. Acts 1:1
2. A. Exod. 18:1
3. B. Ruth 1:3–4
4. B. Esther 1:3, 9
5. A. Acts 18:25
6. A. Judg. 3:12–21
7. B. Acts 24:24
8. C. Jer. 36:1, 23
9. B. Judg. 9:4–5
10. A. Jer. 36:4

QUIZ 2: FISHERS OF MEN
1. B. Mark 3:16
2. A. Mark 2:14
3. C. John 20:25
4. C. The Gospel of John; 1, 2, 3 John; and Revelation
5. C. Matt. 4:18–21
6. A. Mark 3:19
7. A. Acts 12:6–7
8. B. Acts 12:2
9. B. Acts 1:26
10. C. Mark 1:19

QUIZ 3: SPEAKING IN PARABLES
1. C. Matt. 13:33
2. B. Matt. 13:45
3. C. Matt. 13:4
4. A. Luke 15:22
5. B. Matt. 22:3
6. C. Matt. 21:31
7. B. Luke 10:35
8. A. Luke 12:18
9. A. Matt. 20:9
10. B. Luke 19:16–17

QUIZ 4: SEEING AND BELIEVING (JESUS' MIRACLES)
1. C. Matt. 8:24
2. A. Matt. 14:26
3. C. Mark 2:4
4. B. John 11:17
5. B. Mark 5:35
6. C. John 2:3
7. B. Matt. 8:14–15
8. C. Matt. 12:9–13
9. B. Matt. 15:36–38
10. A. Matt. 14:9–21

QUIZ 5: MOTHER LODE
1. C. 2 Sam. 12:14
2. B. Ruth 1:4
3. B. 1 Sam. 1:13
4. C. 1 Sam. 1:20
5. B. Ruth 4:13–17
6. C. Luke 1:76
7. C. 2 Tim. 1:5
8. A. Luke 1:5
9. B. 2 Tim. 1:5
10. C. 1 Chron. 3:5

QUIZ 6: MOTHER LODE
1. C. Gen. 16:8
2. C. Gen. 3:16
3. C. Gen. 16:3
4. B. Luke 2:34
5. A. Gen. 25:20–25
6. B. Gen. 16:10

7. B. Gen. 4:1
8. A. Gen. 20:12
9. C. John 19:26–27
10. A. Gen. 24:1–4, 22, 30

QUIZ 7: PATER PATTER
1. C. Gen. 37:5, 9–10
2. C. Matt. 1:19
3. B. Gen. 29:27–28
4. B. Job 2:9
5. C. Ruth 4:22
6. A. Gen. 11:31
7. A. 1 Sam. 18:27
8. C. Gen. 1:26, 31
9. B. Judg. 11:35
10. A. 1 Chron. 1:1–3

QUIZ 8: SIBLING RIVALRY
1. B. Gen. 16:3–4, 11; 21:9–10
2. C. Exod. 7:10
3. A. Gen. 44:1–2, 12
4. C. Luke 10:39–40
5. A. Gen. 9:22–23, 25
6. C. Gen. 4:16
7. B. Gen. 30:1, 4
8. C. Gen. 33:3
9. C. Num. 12:10, 13
10. A. 2 Sam. 13:1

QUIZ 9: SPLITTING HEIRS
1. B. 1 Kings 21:18–19
2. B. 1 Sam. 20:35–42
3. C. 1 Kings 1:21
4. C. 2 Kings 20:6
5. A. 1 Kings 11:29–31
6. C. 1 Kings 12:17
7. C. 2 Kings 23: 1–3

8. A. 1 Kings 1:11
9. B. 1 Kings 15:13
10. A. 2 Kings 11:1–3

QUIZ 10: WHO'S WHO
1. A. Matt. 17:25, 27
2. B. Acts 5:1–9
3. C. 1 Chron. 10:4
4. A. Gen. 27:43
5. C. Acts 9:17–18
6. B. Dan. 1:7
7. B. John 18:10
8. B. Luke 9:28–36
9. A. Gen. 48:14, 17
10. B. Ezra 5:2; 6:14

QUIZ 11: WATERLOGGED
1. B. Matt. 3:13
2. C. John 4:25
3. C. Exod. 17:6
4. A. Josh. 3:14–15
5. B. Gen. 7:2
6. B. Exod. 7:19–20
7. A. John 9:6–7
8. A. Exod. 13:18
9. C. Gen. 1:10, 13
10. C. Acts 27:27, 41

QUIZ 12: ANGELIC CHORUS
1. B. Luke 1:36
2. B. Luke 2:15
3. A. Luke 1:13
4. A. Gen. 16:8, 11
5. C. Mark 16:5
6. C. Acts 27:23–24
7. C. Gen. 19:1, 11
8. A. Num. 22:27–28, 32
9. C. Dan. 10:5, 21
10. B. Rev. 1:19

MATCH 'EM

QUIZ 13: WHERE THERE'S SMOKE...

1. B. Exod. 3:1–2
2. A. 1 Kings 18:38
3. A. Num. 9:16
4. B. Dan. 3:19
5. C. Exod. 19:18
6. B. Acts 2:3, 6–7
7. B. 2 Kings 2:13
8. C. Lev. 6:12
9. C. Rev. 20:7, 9–10
10. A. Lev. 10:1–2

QUIZ 14: NOTABLE NUMBERS

1. A. Luke 2:42–46
2. B. Luke 4:1–2
3. A. Josh. 4:9
4. B. Num. 13:25
5. B. Rev. 1:4
6. A. Matt. 17:1–4
7. C. Acts 9:8–9
8. C. 1 Sam. 1:1–2
9. B. Exod. 18:25; 24:9
10. C. Exod. 12:2–11

QUIZ 15: CLIMB EVERY ONE

1. C. Gen. 8:4
2. B. Exod. 19:24
3. B. Mark 13:3–37
4. B. 1 Kings 18:20
5. C. 1 Kings 19:8, 11–12
6. C. 2 Sam. 15:14, 30
7. A. 1 Sam. 10:1, 3
8. A. 2 Kings 4:8, 25
9. B. Judg. 4:12–14
10. A. Josh. 12:1

QUIZ 16: POWER IN THE NAME

1. A. Matt. 2:22–23
2. B. Isa. 9:6
3. C. Matt. 9:20–22
4. A. Luke 21:27–28
5. B. Matt. 3:16
6. A. Luke 2:16–18
7. B. Rev. 5:5
8. C. Luke 7:14–15
9. C. Heb. 6:20
10. B. Jer. 23:5

QUIZ 17: YOU SAY ELIJAH...

1. A. 2 Kings 6:5–6
2. C. 1 Kings 17:19–21
3. A. 1 Kings 21:17–21
4. A. 2 Kings 5:9–10
5. B. 2 Kings 4:1, 3
6. C. 1 Kings 18:3
7. B. 1 Kings 17:1
8. B. 2 Kings 5:20–27
9. A. 2 Kings 13:10, 18
10. C. 2 Kings 8:9

QUIZ 18: PEOPLE OF THE CLOTH

1. C. Luke 2:7
2. B. Gen. 3:21
3. B. Mark 1:6
4. C. John 19:23
5. C. Josh. 2:1, 21
6. B. Acts 16:14
7. A. 1 Sam. 1:20; 2:19
8. B. Acts 9:39
9. A. Acts 7:58
10. A. Gen. 27:15–16

BIBLE TRIVIA **CHALLENGE**

QUIZ 19: PROPHETS IN A MINOR KEY

1. C. Jon. 1:15
2. C. Mic. 5:2
3. C. Hosea 1:2
4. B. Mal. 4:5
5. A. Amos 7:8
6. C. Hag. 2:18–19
7. B. Nah. 1:8, 14
8. B. Obad. 1:1
9. A. Zeph. 1:1
10. A. Joel 1:1

QUIZ 20: WHO'S WHO

1. B. Gen. 35:23
2. B. Neh. 2:17
3. C. Acts 8:38
4. B. Matt. 14:6
5. A. John 19:38–39
6. B. Josh. 7:20–21
7. B. Judg. 4:4–5
8. B. John 18:13
9. C. Job 4:1
10. A. Acts 12:25; 13:5

QUIZ 21: TABLE FOR TWO

1. C. Acts 18:2–3
2. C. 2 Sam. 11:14–15
3. A. 1 Sam. 25:23, 25
4. A. Gen. 24:67
5. A. Gen. 31:34
6. B. Gen. 12:10–13; 20:2
7. B. Judg. 16:13, 15
8. C. 1 Sam. 18:27; 2 Sam. 6:23
9. B. Ruth 4:18–21
10. C. Judg. 1:13

QUIZ 22: NOT COUNTING SHEEP

1. A. Matt. 2:13
2. C. Matt. 2:1, 12
3. A. Gen. 28:10, 12
4. C. Gen. 41:25–26
5. A. Gen. 40:22
6. A. Acts 10:13
7. B. Dan. 2:2, 9
8. A. Dan. 2:34
9. C. Dan. 4:19, 22
10. B. Dan. 7:2–3

QUIZ 23: ALSO KNOWN AS

1. C. Gen. 17:5
2. C. Gen. 17:15
3. A. Acts 13:9
4. C. Matt. 4:18
5. A. Gen. 36:1
6. B. Gen. 35:10
7. B. Dan. 1:7
8. B. Dan. 1:7
9. A. Dan. 1:7
10. A. Jer. 20:3

QUIZ 24: FOOD FOR THOUGHT

1. A. Luke 15:27, 31
2. B. Gen. 25:28
3. C. Gen. 25:34
4. B. Num. 13:17, 23
5. A. John 21:13
6. A. Dan. 1:11–12
7. C. Josh. 5:11–12 KJV
8. B. Jer. 24:1
9. C. Isa. 38:21–22
10. B. Gen. 30:15–16

MATCH 'EM

QUIZ 25: THE (SAME) NAME GAME
1. A. Acts 9:11
2. A. 2 Sam. 11:3
3. C. Gen. 39:4
4. A. John 11:2
5. B. John 20:16
6. A. Mark 15:43
7. C. Dan. 1:7; 3:20–21
8. C. 1 Sam. 9:1–2
9. B. Jer. 26:20, 23
10. B. Jer. 28:15

QUIZ 26: NOTABLE NUMBERS
1. A. Num. 13:1–4
2. B. Jer. 25:11
3. B. John 21:2, 11
4. C. Judg. 7:6
5. C. Matt. 1:17
6. A. Gen. 9:29
7. B. Gen. 33:18–19
8. A. Matt. 1:17
9. B. Judg. 9:1–2
10. C. Jer. 32:9

QUIZ 27: HOW GREEN WAS MY...
1. C. John 18:1, 12
2. B. Jer. 19:6
3. A. 1 Sam. 17:2–4
4. C. Judg. 6:33–34
5. B. Judg. 16:4
6. B. 2 Sam. 15:11, 23
7. B. 2 Kings 23:10
8. A. Deut. 2:13–14
9. C. Jer. 19:1–2
10. B. 2 Sam. 5:17–25

QUIZ 28: HOLD FAST
1. C. Matt. 4:2
2. A. Exod. 34:28
3. B. 2 Sam. 12:16
4. B. Acts 14:23
5. B. Matt. 9:14
6. C. 1 Kings 21:27
7. C. 1 Kings 19:8
8. B. Matt. 5:1; 6:17
9. B. Luke 18:10, 12
10. C. Dan. 9:2–3, 21

QUIZ 29: PAGING DR. LUKE
1. B. Matt. 9:20, 22
2. A. Mark 1:30
3. C. Job 2:7
4. C. Num. 12:9–10
5. A. Exod. 9:8–9
6. B. Matt. 8:6
7. A. John 5:1–9, 16
8. B. Luke 17:12, 15
9. C. Acts 28:7–8
10. B. 2 Chron. 26:19, 21

QUIZ 30: WHO'S WHO
1. C. 1 Sam. 17:4
2. A. Luke 3:19–20
3. A. Exod. 2:21
4. A. Acts 19:24, 26
5. C. Esther 3:1
6. B. Ezra 7:1, 13
7. A. 1 Sam. 2:34; 4:11
8. B. Acts 24:27
9. B. Acts 28:1, 7
10. B. 2 Sam. 17:7–14

QUIZ 31: AT REST
1. C. John 19:41
2. A. Gen. 35:16–19

3. B. John 19:38–42
4. C. Gen. 25:8–9
5. B. Gen. 49:33, 50:4–6, 14
6. B. Gen. 35:28–29
7. B. Josh. 24:32
8. B. Gen. 23:1–3, 16
9. A. Deut. 34:5–6
10. C. 2 Sam. 3:32

Quiz 32: Also Known As
1. B. Matt. 9:9; Mark 2:14
2. C. Matt. 12:26–27
3. B. John 1:42
4. A. Num. 13:16
5. A. Ruth 1:20
6. C. Mic. 5:2
7. C. Esther 2:7
8. B. Esther 1:1, kjv
9. C. Judg. 7:1
10. A. Acts 13:6, 8

Quiz 33: The (Same) Name Game
1. A. 1 Sam. 14:22, 26–27
2. B. Mark 14:32–33
3. C. Judg. 4:9
4. B. Gen. 15:2–3
5. A. Acts 15:3–4, 13
6. A. 1 Kings 19:13, 16
7. C. 1 Kings 16:1
8. C. 2 Sam. 15:27
9. C. Exod. 18:2, 4
10. B. Gen. 35:8

Quiz 34: Son of Buzi (Ezekiel)
1. B. Ezek. 1:3
2. C. Ezek. 3:1

3. C. Ezek. 33:7
4. C. Ezek. 4:1, 3
5. A. Ezek. 1:10
6. B. Ezek. 24:2–3
7. A. Ezek. 24:16–18
8. B. Ezek. 9:4, 6
9. A. Ezek. 23:4
10. A. Ezek. 37:16–17

Quiz 35: Reduced to Tears
1. C. John 11:35, 38, 43
2. A. Luke 19:41–44
3. B. 2 Sam. 12:22
4. C. Neh. 1:3–4
5. B. Jer. 38:6
6. A. Jer. 20:2
7. B. Jer. 1:2
8. C. Jer. 27:8, 12
9. B. 2 Kings 8:10–11
10. C. Jer. 13:1

Quiz 36: Double Takes
1. A. Gen. 29:27–28
2. B. Gen. 12:11, 14–15
3. B. 2 Sam. 11:2–3
4. A. 2 Sam. 12:4, 10
5. C. Gen. 35:16, 18
6. C. Esther 2:1–17
7. C. Gen. 20:18
8. A. 1 Sam. 25:18, 20
9. B. Esther 2:5, 7
10. B. 1 Sam. 27:3

Quiz 37: O Jerusalem
1. A. 2 Sam. 5:1, 9
2. B. John 12:12–14
3. C. Neh. 1:3; 6:15

4. A. Luke 4:8–9
5. C. 1 Kings 7:8
6. B. Acts 23:14, 16
7. B. 2 Kings 25:1–21
8. B. Isa. 36:1–8
9. C. Acts 15:1–20
10. A. Rev. 21:22

QUIZ 38: NOTABLE NUMBERS

1. C. Luke 3:23
2. B. Luke 13:4
3. A. Neh. 6:15
4. B. 1 Kings 6:38
5. A. Esther 2:12
6. C. Gen. 23:1–4, 16
7. B. 2 Kings 4:35–36
8. B. Esther 9:12
9. C. Ezek. 4:6
10. A. Ezek. 4:4–5

QUIZ 39: BIRDS OF A FEATHER

1. A. Matt. 3:16
2. B. Luke 2:22–24
3. C. Gen. 8:8–12
4. C. Gen. 1:20–23
5. C. 1 Kings 17:2–4
6. A. Gen. 8:6–7
7. C. Rev. 4:7
8. B. Dan. 4:33
9. B. Lev. 11:13, 16
10. A. Gen. 15:9–10

QUIZ 40: WHO'S WHO

1. A. John 11:1–3
2. A. Jude 9
3. A. Gen. 5:22
4. C. Acts 12:13–14

5. B. Rom. 16:1
6. B. Num. 25:1–9
7. C. Acts 11:28
8. B. 1 Sam. 1:1–2
9. C. Ruth 1:2
10. B. Dan. 2:14

QUIZ 41: CITIES OF REFUGE

1. B. John 2:1–11
2. B. 1 Sam. 16:4, 13
3. C. Matt. 4:12-17
4. B. Acts 11:26
5. A. Acts 9:8, 17–18
6. B. Josh. 6:21, 24, 26
7. C. Gen. 35:1
8. A. Acts 15:40; 16:12–14
9. C. Acts 9:36–41
10. B. Acts 18:18

QUIZ 42: STAFF OF LIFE

1. B. Mark 14:22
2. A. Matt. 4:3
3. B. Ruth 1:3, 6 KJV
4. C. 1 Kings 17:2–6
5. C. Exod. 12:8, 11
6. A. Josh. 5:12
7. B. Exod. 16:21–26
8. C. Lev. 24:5
9. A. Gen. 19:1, 3
10. B. 1 Sam. 21:1, 6

QUIZ 43: TREED

1. B. Gen. 2:15–16; 3:16
2. B. Luke 19:2–4
3. A. Judg. 4:4–5
4. C. Gen. 13:18
5. C. 2 Sam. 18:9

6. A. 1 Kings 7:1, 7
7. C. Judg. 6:11
8. A. 2 Sam. 5:22–23
9. B. Amos 7:14
10. B. Gen. 35:8

QUIZ 44: NOT SAME OLD, SAME OLD

1. B. Exod. 13:18; 14:21–22
2. C. Matt. 3:13–17
3. A. Luke 24:33, 50–51
4. A. Exod. 34:29–32
5. C. Matt. 17:1–2
6. B. Luke 23:33, 45
7. B. Dan. 5:1, 5
8. B. 2 Kings 20:10–11
9. A. Josh. 10:12–13
10. C. Judg. 6:20–21

QUIZ 45: COME AGAIN?

1. B. Acts 10:1 and NIV notes
2. C. John 19:29
3. A. Ruth 2:20
4. C. Exod. 39:1–7
5. B. Acts 6:9
6. A. Ps. 9:16 and NIV note
7. B. Judg. 12:4–7
8. C. Gen. 6:4; Num. 13:33
9. A. Mark 7:11
10. B. 2 Kings 20:11

QUIZ 46: AT SEA (OR RIVER)

1. A. Exod. 2:3
2. C. John 6:1, 16–21
3. A. Rev. 21:2; 22:1
4. B. Gen. 2:10, 14
5. B. Gen. 2:10, 14
6. C. 1 Kings 17:2–4

7. A. Gen. 13:11
8. B. Ezek. 1:3
9. B. Gen. 32:22–30
10. C. Josh. 11:5

QUIZ 47: WITH A SONG IN MY HEART

1. C. Luke 2:8–14
2. A. Luke 1:39–55
3. B. Exod. 15:1–18
4. A. Num. 21:17
5. B. Deut. 31:16, 19
6. A. Judg. 5:1
7. B. 1 Sam. 1:27–2:10
8. B. Luke 2:27–32
9. C. Rev. 15:2–4
10. C. Rev. 5:8–10

QUIZ 48: THE PERILS OF PAUL

1. B. Acts 13:2, 5
2. C. Acts 13:6
3. B. Acts 15:40; 16:3
4. A. Acts 16:12, 23
5. C. Acts 18:1–2
6. C. Acts 19:1, 11–12
7. B. Acts 20:7–12
8. A. Acts 21:17; 22:24–29
9. B. Acts 27:13–14
10. C. Acts 28:1, 5

QUIZ 49: TIES THAT BIND

1. B. Exod. 4:14
2. C. Gen. 16:15; 21:2
3. C. Gen. 4:25
4. A. Gen. 30:12–13
5. C. 2 Sam. 4:4
6. B. Gen. 25:26; 30:19–21

7. A. Gen. 30:23–24; 35:16; 41:51–52
8. B. Ruth 4:17, 22; 2 Sam. 13:1
9. A. 2 Sam. 5:13–14
10. C. 2 Sam. 8:16

QUIZ 50: WHO'S WHO
1. A. Josh. 2:1
2. B. Matt. 26:57–65
3. B. 2 Chron. 36:22–23
4. A. Numbers 16
5. C. Acts 6:1–5
6. C. Acts 16:22–40
7. B. Book of Philemon
8. C. 1 Kings 2:13–22
9. B. Dan. 1:3
10. C. Acts 27:1, 43

QUIZ 51: THE (SAME) NAME GAME
1. A. John 13:26
2. A. Acts 8:30–35
3. B. Gen. 26:7–10
4. A. 2 Tim. 4:14
5. B. Matt. 15:33; Jude 1:1
6. B. Exod. 6:25–26
7. C. 1 Sam. 7:1
8. A. Judg. 8:28–31
9. C. Matt. 14:3
10. B. Acts 4:1–7

QUIZ 52: CITIES OF REFUGE
1. C. Matt. 2:19–23
2. C. Acts 17:22–23
3. A. Luke 24:50
4. C. Gen. 23:1–2, 19
5. A. Judg. 16:21–30

6. B. 1 Sam. 1:19–20
7. C. 1 Kings 19:1–3
8. C. Matt. 15:21–28
9. B. Acts 18:2
10. B. Josh. 14:13

QUIZ 53: BIRTH OF A NATION (ABRAHAM'S JOURNEY)
1. B. Gen. 11:27–28
2. C. Gen. 11:31–32
3. A. Gen. 12:6
4. B. Gen. 12:8
5. A. Gen. 12:10
6. C. Gen. 12:14, 17
7. A. Gen. 13:10–11
8. B. Gen. 13:18
9. A. Gen. 14:17
10. B. Gen. 14:18–20

QUIZ 54: A PROMISE IS A PROMISE
1. C. Gen. 9:13–17
2. A. Gen. 12:7
3. B. Gen. 18:1, 10
4. B. Gen. 28:13–14
5. B. 2 Chron. 1:11–12
6. A. Matt. 11:28
7. B. John 3:16
8. A. Gen. 3:15
9. C. Matt. 19:28
10. A. 2 Sam. 7:16

QUIZ 55: ALSO KNOWN AS
1. A. Matt. 1:23
2. C. Isa. 14:12–15 KJV
3. A. Gen. 14:3 and Bible maps

4. A. Biblical notes and NIV notes
5. C. Acts 9:36
6. C. Acts 12:12
7. B. Isaiah 20 and Bible maps
8. C. 1 Kings 14:21; 2 Chron. 26:1
9. B. 2 Sam. 12:24–25
10. B. 2 Kings 24:17

Quiz 56: Just about Jesus
1. B. Matt. 4:8–9
2. A. Matt. 8:31
3. C. Matt. 16:1, 4
4. A. John 4:4–5
5. B. Matt. 10:1
6. B. John 2:13–17; Matt. 21:12–13
7. B. John 10:32–33
8. A. Matt. 5:5
9. C. Josh. 6:22–25; Matt. 1:5
10. C. Matt. 11:21–23

Quiz 57: Passion Week
1. B. Matt. 21:1–11
2. B. Mark 14:1–3
3. B. Matt. 26:14–16
4. C. John 19:31
5. C. Mark 14:32, 41
6. B. Matt. 28:5–7
7. A. Mark 14:13
8. C. Mark 11:11–17
9. C. Mark 14: 43–45
10. A. John 18:12–13

Quiz 58: Welcome Wagon
1. A. Genesis 18
2. B. Gen. 19:1–4

3. A. Gen. 24:26–31
4. C. Exod. 2:15–20
5. A. Job 42:11
6. C. 1 Sam. 9:18–24
7. C. Neh. 5:17–18
8. A. 2 Sam. 6:12–19
9. B. Judg. 13:15–16
10. B. 3 John 1–8

Quiz 59: Ties That Bind
1. A. Luke 1:59–60
2. C. Esther 2:7
3. C. Judges 13
4. B. Gen. 24:15
5. A. Esther 5:10
6. B. 2 Sam. 6:3
7. A. Gen. 4:19–21
8. B. Lev. 10:16
9. C. 1 Sam. 4:18–21
10. C. Num. 27:1

Quiz 60: Who's Who
1. C. John 19:19
2. C. 1 Sam. 1:10–11
3. A. Acts 11:25–26
4. A. 2 Sam. 18:1–16
5. B. Acts 16:1–3
6. A. 1 Sam. 14:50
7. B. 2 Kings 8:7–15
8. B. 1 Sam. 26:6–9
9. C. Gen. 19:36–38
10. A. 2 Cor. 2:12–13